LISTENING FOR GOD'S VOICE
(Meditations, Memoirs, Personal Essays, and Poetry)

DONNA COLLIER RICKMAN

WESTBOW
PRESS®
A DIVISION OF THOMAS NELSON
& ZONDERVAN

This book is a work of non-fiction. Unless otherwise noted, the author and the publisher make no explicit guarantees as to the accuracy of the information contained in this book and in some cases, names of people and places have been altered to protect their privacy.

WestBow Press books may be ordered through booksellers or by contacting:

WestBow Press
A Division of Thomas Nelson & Zondervan
1663 Liberty Drive
Bloomington, IN 47403
www.westbowpress.com
844-714-3454

Because of the dynamic nature of the Internet, any web addresses or links contained in this book may have changed since publication and may no longer be valid. The views expressed in this work are solely those of the author and do not necessarily reflect the views of the publisher, and the publisher hereby disclaims any responsibility for them.

Any people depicted in stock imagery provided by Getty Images are models, and such images are being used for illustrative purposes only. Certain stock imagery © Getty Images.

Scripture quotations are taken from the King James Version, unless otherwise stated.

Lighthouse image by Mary Lynne Richards

ISBN: 978-1-6642-8854-6 (sc)
ISBN: 978-1-6642-8856-0 (hc)
ISBN: 978-1-6642-8855-3 (e)

Library of Congress Control Number: 2023900206

Print information available on the last page.

WestBow Press rev. date: 3/14/2023

FOREWORD

It has been my pleasure to serve as a spiritual guide and Bible assistant to my beloved and anointed wife in the construction of this work. We, at all times have considered the uplifting value of the contents and pray that people will find help in the thoughts expressed herein.

Through her writings, the reader may experience clarity and resolution to their questions. Her style of writing takes the reader directly to the eventful happenings. I believe the reading of this collection will develop a closer bond between the reader and God.

Further, it is the author's hope as she has expressed to me, that readers will benefit in their own lives from her sharing many of her own trials and tribulations. Also, by the help of God, via His voice and appointed angels... she has overcome most of her challenges, gained strength and discernment and learned to enjoy everyday living.

Dennis Rickman

IN MEMORIAM

To my beloved husband, Dennis Vandeleur Rickman, who passed from this life unto eternity (God's Kingdom) on September 9, 2022. His words of love and support are radiated throughout this book like the lighthouses on the pages and I thank him.

Donna Collier Rickman

INTRODUCTION

<u>What the Author Hopes to Convey in the Book:</u>

This book is a collection of inspirational writings as heard by the author from God's voice. Since the age of twelve when she first gave herself to God through Jesus Christ at Eighth and Center Street Baptist Church in Hannibal, Missouri (her hometown) she has sensed His Holy presence in her life. Through the years, God has touched her life in so many ways; literally, "breaking shackles neath a load of guilt and shame" to allow her favor in listening for His guiding voice.

To the best of her abilities through the workings of the Holy Spirit, she has tried to breathe God's word into the writing of each entry from experiences and challenges faced by herself and characters within the Bible using various themes which are cited in alphabetical order. Hopefully, through such design these themes can aid the readers and soothe their hearts in what they are soulfully seeking in a word from God as they magnify His Holy name.

Had it not been for the Lord, she is not sure that she or they would have survived such situations; spiritually, mentally and physically. In most cases, we have triumphed and overcome both unforeseen and seen obstacles head on. Others, she has found are slowly brewing as she finds herself still working via professional therapy and medications. However, as a witness to His divineness, miracles, and glory... she knows that God stays close by and dwells within her spirit.

Also, there exists ripples of hilarity in some of these works which allows the reader some opportunities to reflect back to a softer time and melodious journey in his or her sojourn with God, thus enjoying the simpler things in life and laughing with thanksgiving about how you got over with God's grace. To God be the glory throughout your reading!

How To Read This Book:

This book comprises a collection of inspirational writings and poetry as heard by the author from listening for God's voice to direct her steps throughout this writing venture. Most often, she wants the reader to think about the lighthouses on the covers and throughout the pages to meditate on the serenity, solace, and spirituality which they can offer and that she found her hometown lighthouse afforded her.

She has written a religiously-oriented non-fiction book which contains entries written in memoirs, personal essays, Christian meditations, and selected self-written poems. Meditations have originated from characters using primarily the King James Version along with other versions of the Bible and tell how they evolved in their relationships with the Lord as the writer has successfully conveyed to her readers.

She has designated a group of scriptures to pre-read prior to each anticipated entry. They in turn will intertwine with each writing but are listed under Further Reading toward the end of the book. She then selectively places each entry under twenty-one themes upon which they are grouped accordingly.

This makes it easier to select a reading for a specific need or concern which one might have and wants to find out how the character(s) made it through and possibly, open the doors for readers to journal and share their own experiences as well under such themes.

In finality, she closes each entry with a revelation, endeavor, and prayer to use in one's daily living. Throughout the entries, she has allowed the reader the opportunity to relate and reflect upon the scriptural passages and find meaning in the substance and settings of her writings.

ACKNOWLEDGEMENTS

My daughter, Maggie for her undying technical assistance prior to manuscript submission. My son, Mark Jr. for the gift of a new computer to type my manuscript. My late husband, Dennis for his spiritual clarity, enlightenment, advisory, daily dialogue, and sounding board assistance regarding the Bible as a past Sunday School and Bible Study Teacher.

Faye Green Dant and Rhonda Brown Hall for resource helps and knowledge of African-American History and Culture in Hannibal, Missouri; Hallie Yundt Silver, Director of the Hannibal Public Free Library for contacts, older pictures and news articles as they related to The Mark Twain Memorial Lighthouse. Mary Lynne Richards, Parks and Recreation Department in Hannibal, Missouri, for her consent to use her photographs of the lighthouse.

My friend, Ranee Dukes for her Christian sisterhood and insight, my cousin, Desiree Battle for her continuous spiritual support and my church, New Covenant AME Community Church, for their prayers and well wishes in this endeavor. Also, Pastor Barbara Brown for her theological discernment and overview of this book.

My copy editor, Mike Valentino, for his professional editing services.

DEDICATION

To the memory of my late parents, James and Virginia Collier for their love, perseverance, and sacrifices given throughout their lives to keep our family intact and knowing and serving Jesus Christ.

EPIGRAPH
LISTENING FOR GOD'S VOICE

"Lord, I have done my duty and I have told
the truth and kept nothing back."
Sojourner Truth

CONTENTS

ANXIOUSNESS

DISOBEDIENCE

EXALTATION

FAITH

FORGIVENESS

FREEDOM

GRACE

HOPE

JOY

LOVE

LOYALTY

MARRIAGE

OBEDIENCE

PATIENCE

PEACE

PERSEVERANCE

REASSURANCE

SACRIFICE

STRENGTH

TRUST

WISDOM

POETRY

POETIC JOURNEYING

Barren, bleak and blundering moments
spent silently journeying,
has harvested and reaped for this lone traveler...
powerfully- plain, poetic justice
of lyricism in the rye.
Written by Donna Collier Rickman

ANXIOUSNESS

(Extreme Uneasiness or Fear
About Something or Someone)

LISTLESS MOODS

My soul melteth for heaviness: strengthen
thou me according unto thy word.

PSALM 119:28

"Bless the Lord, oh my soul and all that is within me, bless His Holy name!" Psalm 103:1. My soul melteth for heaviness. Strengthen me oh Lord. Everyday living and life's trials can place such a heavy burden on us. Where can we go to catch a break? A break from all of the chaos and listlessness of the world's troubles and uncertainties; homelessness and disease; lack of job security and affordable health care; poverty and suffering; injustice and brutality; assaults and violence; senseless killings and unwarranted freedoms?

"Where is God in all of this?" How does anything make sense anymore and what is the world coming to? Jesus taught us to come to Him and He would give us rest. But what about our souls; the very core of our foundation and the essence of our being? When our minds, hearts and souls feel such heaviness so profoundly deep, how do we resolve to let go and let God handle it and allow Him to strengthen us? What do we say and what should we do about all of our anxiousness?

We must allow our Heavenly Father to strengthen us according to His word. We must learn to listen for His still, calming voice to instill some normalcy and decency amidst the frenzy of our pages. We are enormously overwhelmed and feeling shut down in helplessness and hopelessness. Our only answer is to somehow submit and allow the Master to intervene on our behalf. We must just close our inner beings off from the outside world and all of its distractions to embrace all that our Heavenly Father longs for us to hear and understand.

Unless or until we invite God into the picture, we remain as victims, vulnerable to the atrocities of this world which leaves us yearning for both truth and strength. Truth to examine and know that He is Almighty God and will truly never leave us alone in all of our grief and bewilderment. Strength to get up, fight back, persevere, and recover our lost souls with the solace of peace of mind, hope, grace, and mercy from our Maker above versus mere anxiousness.

In light of everything going on, how will we mentally survive, rather than becoming plagued with major depression and overwhelming anxiety? If we basically feel cast down on every side, how will we replenish our strength to muster another day to make a comeback? How will we survive another takedown if we don't have the will to survive as there are already high rates of mental illness amongst us? What must we do to hear Your voice of healing, dear Father, as we speak out and scream Your name?

Revelation: In our daily struggles, we need to let go and let God do for us in spite of the mood of our nation and the heaviness of our hearts.

Endeavor: May we remember to hold fast daily to God in all of our triumphs as well as trials.

Prayer: Please forgive us our trespasses as we trespass against you, oh Lord, even in our anxiousness and give us strength. For it is You who provides us sustenance of our daily bread. And for that, we are most humbled and thankful. Amen.

WANDERING SPIRIT

*Be careful for nothing; but in everything by
prayer and supplication with thanksgiving let
your requests be made known unto God.*

PHILIPPIANS 4:6

My husband and I purchased an 1894 Victorian home. I will never forget; we were just so elated about the nuances of our new home as we knew it was God sent! Not our making but the Lord's doing in our lives as we had prayed on this for some time and finally, lo and behold, it revealed itself. We humbly thanked God for His marvelous blessing.

Many times, we would hold morning devotionals reading from the Bible accompanied by auxiliary materials to support the scriptures for the day. Likewise, we would write such scriptures down and refer back to them on another day.

Our house had an electrical system that, according to the appraiser, was not up to par for the long haul. At least not through thirty years of our habitation in light of our mortgage. He asserted that we would probably be looking at updating the whole system someday. We figured, that that was many moons away, so our minds wandered way into the future.

Then, one day out of the blue on a cold winter's early morn, the breaker tripped. Suddenly, no lights, no heat, no electricity period. Our minds swirled all over the place and we began panicking about the cost to install a newly rebuilt system. We didn't remember it, but just the night before I had written down the verse above from Philippians about "wanting for nothing and through all prayer and supplication with thanksgiving, let our requests be known unto the Lord." Certainly, we had done that!

When the electrician first came, he had to assess the problem. After his return, he brought along a lone circuit breaker. Upon installation - much to our amazement - everything started up! He told us that it was only one of two that could be found for its age. What we thought was going to cost thousands of dollars was only $70.00 total including the service!

Do we sometimes become impatient with holding on to God's word? Are we then left with a wandering spirit of doubt? Do we often fail to truly release and let God do whatever He will do? Or, do we think the worst in light of our situation? Should we say, "Not our will, but yours, Lord?"

Revelation: Make known God's truth in our paths.

Endeavor: Let us always humbly give thanks for all of our blessings.

Prayer: Help us to make our requests clearly known to you, oh Lord, knowing that we can do all things through Christ Who gives us wisdom and most importantly, strength! So, there is no need to be anxious when you remember that God is at the helm. Amen.

SOJOURNING ANOTHER DAY

Beloved, think it not strange concerning the fiery trial which is to try you, as though some strange thing happened unto you: But rejoice, inasmuch as ye are partakers of Christ's sufferings; that when his glory shall be revealed, ye may be glad also with exceeding joy.

I PETER 4:12-13

Teaching had become my later life career in my mid-thirties after having gone back to school acquiring my Associate's in Psychology and Bachelor's in School education (certified K-12) and Community Health Education short of my Master's in Elementary Education through Middle School Education with an emphasis in science. Previously, I had worked as a paraprofessional in health care and even worked an internship followed by a community health educator position at the county health department prior to classroom teaching.

So, when I finally made the transition to teaching in the public schools, I did just that. First, I took a Substitute Teaching position at a rural high school. Following, I worked in both suburban and urban school districts while working the following positions through the city's community college, a rural college, the area math and science center and area churches: Talented and Gifted Program teaching elementary sciences and math; Upward Bound Program teaching urban high school students Biology and Environmental sciences; Coordinated the Saturday Academy Program, an educational program for high school students of color with emphasis on math, sciences, writing, and College

Prep courses, and Diverse Outreach Conferences for fifth-grade girls in the sciences and math at a rural college.

Therefore, thanks to my certifications, I could be assigned to work from elementary, middle and high school classrooms in any school district. On one particular assignment, my assignment was split: two-thirds of my assignment at the high school and the other third at a middle school. I was excited to be able to teach Health education at both levels.

It was different to rotate between both the buildings at first although I had previously taught at a middle school teaching three different subjects, but I was willing, able-bodied, and anticipating any and all challenges. It was a great feeling to see how the curriculum which I taught to the middle schoolers would then follow in my work with the high school students afterwards. I just knew that I had found my niche in education and thoroughly enjoyed making the connections across the curricula.

Then, one day the unthinkable happened. I found myself as an educator caught between two female high school students who had a bone to pick, however not just between themselves but with me as well. I was caught in the middle of them both and believe me, they took their angst out not just on each other but on me as well as I was hit on both sides and knocked down to the floor. It was to the point that my head hit a heater, six students jumped into the scrum with me in the middle and my body was literally picked up and moved by a male student to another place on the floor. God had sent my major angel that day.

Soon, a fellow educator came in and picked me up from the floor helping me onto my feet after literally feeling the ruckus on his classroom floor next door. He was another angel present that day who came and found me and secured me away. Students later told me that although my eyes were open, I seemed listless to reality at that time. I did not respond when they tried to speak to me. Six students were sent to the nurse's office for cuts, bruises, and physical clashes. It was a real mess!

But I had the nerve to stand behind my podium and ask the class why nobody helped me. It was then that they informed me of their many services performed on my behalf that day as other angels. I could not personally ascertain all that had occurred as I was detached for a good deal of the altercations.

I tried to come back to work the next day, but had been experiencing such pain, swollenness, stress, and shame that I could not function and cried all of the time. I told the principal at my middle school assignment what had happened and how I was also experiencing much pain and was depressed. I ended up getting the Educational Association and local teacher's union involved to the point where I went to the police station and filed assault charges against the two girls. It turned out that I had suffered a dislocated jaw along with various contusions throughout my body.

To top it off, I was diagnosed with Post-Traumatic Stress Disorder (PTSD) filled with major depression and chronic anxiety. I was feeling helpless and hopeless, totally distraught. And the feeling of shame I could not shake. I attended the criminal hearing for both students. They were expelled and put into a different program outside of the high school they had been attending and could not graduate with their class. As for me, I could not teach for months and was placed on medical leave with a program for revitalizing both my mental and physical health as I set forth sojourning another day of living.

All of what happened seemed like a nightmare for months. Even though I went through the fiery furnace, I had not a reason for why and could not understand the lesson I was supposed to have learned in all of it. It was a very strange out of body experience to be a part of and one I hoped would never happen again... although the PTSD did return again some nine years later. I cannot say that I thanked God for the experience, however I did thank Him time and time again for my deliverance and persistence to want to teach and educate children still because of the love I had for them. However, I was given the opportunity to come back to reality and rejoice in God's gift of teaching from my first experience of PTSD which I truly embraced and loved sojourning another day.

Have you ever found yourself in a position which you could not easily break through? Did you ask God for deliverance? Did you get the physical and/or mental health services needed for survival, or just take the situation for what you thought it was worth and do nothing? Can we learn to live again despite memories of defeat and everything becoming a desolate mess amid the bright shining glory of the Lord availing itself as we question why about our situation?

Revelation: Sometimes, we need to just be still and look for all of the angels sent to help us on our behalf.

Endeavor: May we remember Your sufferings on the cross, Heavenly Father, as you remember us, Your children through our sufferings yet, rejoice in Your glory.

Prayer: Let us look to you, the Lord our God, from whence all of our help and answers come when we least expect them in all of our anxiousness. Please remind us constantly as to who You are in relationship to our daily lives. Thanks for sending Your many angels in the times of need to help us through our trials and tribulations as we never know when they might come. Amen.

DELICATE EYES

Fear thou not; for I am with thee: be not dismayed; for I am thy God: I will strengthen thee; yea, I will help thee; yea, I will uphold thee with the right hand of my righteousness.

ISAIAH 41:10

Eyes are truly the windows into one's soul. There is nothing like them and to be minus one's eyes is to be minus a part of one's soul because of both the beautiful and ugly that can be seen, recognized, and remembered via our vision...our memories. A true treasure or storehouse of memory all unlocked via our most delicate eyes. Yet, it is absolutely amazing how God Himself, enhances the other vital senses for those who otherwise, lose one or both eyes literally or become blinded in one or both eyes either through conception, birth or another way and lose their sight for life.

I can remember these instances which could have affected both of my eyes at different times like they happened yesterday, plus my current situation. In around 2008, I had been working in my rock garden digging fairly deep into the ground when I felt a fingernail bend backwards against a rock. It most definitely hit hard. As a matter of fact, I had not expected to find a rock down so deep. I had removed my gardening gloves for some reason that I can't remember. In any event, my left eyelid started itching, so I scratched it a couple of times thinking nothing of my actions.

Several days later, I began to have problems seeing out of my left eye. The lid had become swollen and had closed over my eye. I called my optometrist, and was able to get in almost immediately. Upon seeing me, the doctor diagnosed me with cellulitis and admitted me into the hospital. Blood work was drawn and it turned out that I had contracted (MRSA) methicillin-resistant Staphylococcus aureus in my left eye. After cultures and observation, it turned out that it was not directly found in the eyeball but crevices of my eyelid.

In any event, I underwent 4-5 days of enduring a swollen eyelid that took on a rectangular shape filled with infection as I was set-up in an isolated room. Finally, one evening the doctor came in along with the nurse both carrying vials, Lidocaine, syringes, and other surgical gauze talking about how he was going to remove the infection from out of my eyelid.

I had never felt such uncomfortableness in my life. One of my hands clung onto the nurse's hand while my other hand held on for dear life on the rail. I felt like I was gushing sweats. For what just took moments, I swear lasted a lifetime in minutes as I screamed and cried for my dear life. I prayed that I wouldn't lose my eye in all of this. Everything seemed so closed in a very tight space.

Finally, the doctor said that he was all done and I witnessed the substance from my eye all in the gauze on the steel plate on my table. The Lidocaine seemed worthless. Luckily, the doctor stated that the MRSA had no chance to drain down into my eye from its lid or move upward into my brain. I remember feeling so relieved, yet still traumatized from the surgical procedure. Within the next day or two, I was discharged and freed from the bondage of wretched fear which I had felt in all of this. My husband and I thanked God and praised Him for His gift of my eye. I remember just praying thankfulness for days on end as I was so frightened.

Then most recently in February of 2021, I had visited an ophthalmologist referred by my optometrist's office for problems associated this time with my right eye and a shooting pain from my head that seemed to be entering my optic nerve and going into my eyeball. She took notes and asked me seemingly a thousand questions. Then, she had me to go to the lab to have blood work drawn.

I didn't find out the next day, but the second day after that I was due to have out-patient surgery as my labs proved abnormal and showed that

I had inflammation in my body that was very high. She got in touch with a vascular surgeon who thought that I was experiencing problems with Giant Cell Arteritis which could result from inflammation found in both temporal arteries of my head. Now, the vascular surgeon wanted to perform biopsies on both arteries to rule out such a diagnosis. I could suffer a stroke in one or both of my eyes so the situation was serious.

Throughout the ordeal of waiting for both biopsies, I admit that my faith had waned and I was scared to death. The thought of losing my eyesight was devastating. I experienced many restless and lonely nights frightened by such a diagnosis and the thought of being on more than the 80 mgs of a steroid which the doctor had immediately prescribed for me rocked my soul. I felt totally helpless waiting for my results.

I called upon God many times however, my faith was fruitless as Satan constantly tried to deprive me of the great Divine and His healing words of peace and comfort until the third night when I just released myself and gave my burden to Christ. I felt a sweet, childlike comfort from my Father as He swaddled me in my comforter and seemed to hold me like a baby. At those defining moments, I knew God was present because I let Him in and let Him fight my battle as I felt His most gentle touch. It was like He rocked me to sleep.

I actually heard God tell me not to be afraid. That He had been with me all along and would fight my battles, strengthen and help me so as, not to be dismayed and He would uphold me with His right hand of righteousness. Then, I got the phone call the next day and the nurse said both biopsies were clear. I started ministering to her on the phone and praising the Lord giving Him all the honor, glory, and praise. Following, I called up family and friends and told them the good news as well as to how God had saved my eyes!

Now, I am facing my newest tribulation with my right eye. It is all dependent upon the condition of my Lacrimal gland. Currently, it is swollen and can be seen as such if one takes their finger and pushes open wide the eyeball in the upper right orbital area of the eye socket. I have not yet met with the surgeon, but my ophthalmologist recommends a biopsy on the Lacrimal gland. I am not scheduled for an evaluation until early June as I may possibly have other needed surgical work on my eyelids done as well.

I have been waiting since February to see the surgeon. Now, it is May 2021. The problem lies in what the biopsy reveals as the problem. A viral or bacterial infection, various eye disorders, or worse yet, a condition in which I can't even fathom… let alone say. All I can do is wait at this time as I do believe the Lord will once again, intervene and give me peace of mind, body, and spirit. I have to admit, I am not the strongest Christian around during these times and still have nights of unrest wondering about this whole situation.

Also, I have to admit that I will be glad when my gland is assessed and biopsied for me to find out the reason behind the swelling of it and what, if anything I can do to stop the other gland from swelling as well. At times, I suffer from what feels like a migraine in my right eye. I take Ibuprofen 400mg and that calms it down as I lie awake in the dark of the night. Lord knows that I spin into a fear which I cannot describe as I begin having all kinds of wavering thoughts. I pray to the Lord and ask Him to forgive my doubts and/or misgivings as I consciously bat my eyelids to stay abreast of my situation feeling my eyes.

Several days pass and it is my appointment with the surgeon specialist. The night proved brutal initially, but soon I calmed down and was able to sleep during increments of time. Almost any possible scenario I think of may happen upon my appointment. I tremble at the realization of my moments soon to come. My ophthalmologist has made me fathom the worst diagnoses of biopsy and surgery along with Google and other informational media as my son drives me to my appointment over an hour away at the university medical center for specialty care.

Finally, the time is here. I meet the surgical specialist. She prods and examines until finally coming to her assessments. I don't need to have a biopsy on my Lacrimal gland after all. It is indeed swollen… enlarged but not much different from other patients whom she has examined previously to me with one gland being larger than the other. She felt no tumors as I so dreaded that she'd find nor deemed any other diagnosis present. My droopy eye syndrome she felt could wait longer for surgery and she had her technician take about seven pictures of my face and eyes for future reference in case of changes down the road.

I was so overjoyed yet felt so deflated at the news that I could barely praise the Lord. I had been so frightened and uncertain about the possible loss of my eyesight that I was almost rendered speechless. I remember that during check-out, I still felt listless and somewhat overwhelmed by the resurgence of everything upon me. Possibly, I was in shock. Certainly, I welcomed the surgeon's news but was still feeling confounded and at a loss for words. I had carried such a weight for over three months until today.

Most definitely, Satan had been robbing me of my blessings and God's manifest glory, divine healing and omnificent mercy. Part of it was me lost in the maze of man's diagnosis and not the Lord's will I admit. But I just felt so isolated, so separated from the Lord during those times. I thank Him for getting me through another day's journey keeping me sheltered under His wings of protection and care. I now have a renewed sense of salvation found in the Lord because I know that He forever held my hand.

Have you ever felt helpless to the point of being defeated in your abilities to truly serve and reverence the Lord? Did it seem at times that you were alone in the fight for your life? Did you need reassurance from the Lord that He was indeed present in your life and had been all along? When your natural means of serving and praising the Lord became reality, what did you do then?

Revelation: Know that God stands by us and upholds us as He strengthens us with His right hand of righteousness as we forever lean upon Him.

Endeavor: We should forever remember the Lord and hold steadfast to His unchanging hands and be not dismayed or ultimately shaken, anxious, and defeated despite or in spite of our very human fears as we grow in the Lord's promises.

Prayer: Like doubting Thomas, we need to ask the Lord to forgive our humanness filled with woes, fears, and concerns which we may feel from time to time versus fully trusting in Him under all circumstances at all times. He is after all, our ultimate Way-Maker! Amen.

DISOBEDIENCE

(Refusal Or Neglect To Obey Or
Conform Or Comply With Something)

IGNORANT DECISIONS

And thine ears shall hear a word behind thee, saying,
This is the way, walk ye in it, when ye turn to the
right hand, and when ye turn to the left.

ISAIAH 30:21

I shall never forget that after entering the seventh grade, I wanted to be and do everything like my older sister who was then in high school. So, from the very moment she awoke each morning to her bedtime at night, I was caught up in idolizing my big sister.

She was a natural beauty with big, oval shaped, medium brown colored eyes and a beautiful smile with glowing teeth. I adored everything about her. The way she rolled her hair on pink foam rollers to the styling of her curls; from brushing her teeth to the ironing and wearing of her clothes for school, play, and church. But the biggest thrill for me was her wearing stockings and how she pulled them up… attaching them to her garter belt.

All I wanted was to one day, be emboldened enough, courageous enough, and obstinate enough to dare… let alone actually wear her undergarments and stockings to school. I waited but heard no word from the Lord that I was in the wrong. No ignorant decision here.

She had to be at the bus stop before me to ride to the high school. Then, one morning, I did it. I snuck her garments on under my dress. I used safety pins to crease, make double folds and hold the garter belt around my hips. Soon, we leave for the bus stop and my brother doesn't seem to notice my wearing stockings on my legs. I praise myself for a good job.

The driver pulls up in front of the school and I stand up. Suddenly, I feel a most unusual sensation and find everything buckling, then rushing down my legs practically to my ankles. Believe me, I could hear the Lord talking to me as I was getting all kinds of admonishments and corrections in my ears to walk if not trot off that bus.

I hear the bus driver tell kids to stay seated as my brother escorts me off the bus and shields me behind the bushes. Literally, I have to pick the stockings and garter belt up from the ground to run to the bushes. It is funny years later but certainly wasn't at the time. My sister cracks up from hearing this story.

Do we too often listen to the wrong thoughts and find ourselves in precarious positions? What can we do once we have made such decisions in haste? Did we really hear the voice of God? Or, was it our own selfish reasons to inflate our egos? Should we really let go of our own radar for decency in our life choices?

Revelation: Acknowledge the Lord at all times and give Him the glory.

Endeavor: May we learn to listen for an ever deeper meaning in God's voice.

Prayer: Deliver us from our ignorant decisions often made in haste. Remind us that we must give You the glory and keep You first despite worldly temptations. And when we feel overwhelmed in the midst of it all, let us simply pray and ask for forgiveness from all unrighteousness. Amen.

NOT MY BROTHER'S KEEPER

And Cain talked with Abel his brother: and it came to pass, when they were in the field, that Cain rose up against Abel his brother, and slew him. And the Lord said unto Cain, where is Abel thy brother? And he said, I know not: Am I my brother's keeper?

GENESIS 4: 8-9

Abel a keeper of sheep and Cain a tiller of the ground were probably designated such jobs and skills by God Himself as He invested in their on-the-job training and guided them through the processes toward success.

Cain's offering to the Lord was fruit of the ground, but it was seen as unacceptable to the Lord as he did not show respect in the Lord's eyes, maybe as it related to their mother and father Adam and Eve and their partaking of the forbidden fruit in the garden. Thus, he became angry and despondent in spirit as his facial expression changed. Abel's offering to the Lord was accepted and he was highly praised as he probably gloated in pride and favor from the Lord. He yielded unto the Lord baby sheep with their tender and succulent fat.

It seems that while the brothers were yet in the field, something terrible and repulsive came over Cain to the point of him outrightly killing his brother Abel. Immediately, the Lord must have felt the dagger as He asked Cain about his brother's whereabouts. In turn Cain said he did not know as he was not his brother's keeper. But the Lord knew that Abel's blood had been spilled by Cain's hands all over the earth inhabiting the cracks in the ground in their field.

Following, the Lord issued His sentence upon Cain saying no longer would the ground yield her full harvest of crops and fruits for him and he shall be known as a fugitive killer and vagabond upon the earth no matter where he travelled. The exception in this case would be for any and all who wanted to kill Cain. Then God would put His mark upon him not to do so, however, if one did kill him, vengeance from the Lord would be put out on him sevenfold or seven times the initial expectation.

This story tells the lesson of our Lord who knew everything from the simplest to most complex happenings as He was the maker and creator of everything great and small. Just as He had previously discerned the problem with Adam and Eve, so did He know about the confrontation between the brothers and their sure end. This had the likes of pure hatred, envy, jealousy and venomous anger projected in a need to kill looming in its wake.

This is a lesson to be learned for all of God's children who proclaim Him as Lord and Savior in our lives. In many cases and circumstances, we can get on our knees and ask for repentance from our sins. However, killing in self-defense or for such a time as in life and death during the combat in war are two different situations not in effect here. For even in the Bible, Ecclesiastes 3:3, it talks about a "time to kill."

Even within this twenty-first century, we must be cognizant of our actions toward every human life. Sadly enough, not everyone who kills is found guilty of their trespasses and put into prison to pay for their crime or given a death sentence. However, we will all have to answer to God at the end of our lives for whatever choices we have made in our daily lives.

Have we ever been a witness to death and what did we do about it afterwards in victim advocacy? How often has our anger come to the boiling point and how did we handle its circumstances? What can be so horrific to make one kill his sibling or any other fellow human being in cold blood? Do we truly understand the consequences of our actions?

Revelation: Make ourselves accountable keeping a check on our spurts of anger.

Endeavor: Let the Lord, our Savior see the goodness in His children and flock and be proud still!

Prayer: Enable us to become our brother's and sister's keepers and provide support to those in need. Allow us to develop special relationships with our family members, particularly our siblings regarding all things. Amen.

LOST AT SEA

Now the Lord hath prepared a great fish to swallow up
Jonah. And Jonah was in the belly of the fish three days
and three nights. Then Jonah prayed unto the Lord his
God out of the fish's belly. And the Lord spake unto the
fish, and it vomited out Jonah upon the dry land.

JONAH 1:17; 2:1,10

Our Lord God knows everything we do or ever hope to do, plan, and
work in our lifetimes. Basically, we can run from our transgressions, but
we can't hide as He is so ever aware of all of our thoughts and intentions;
good, bad, and indifferent to His plans for our lives.

Since He created us, He knows our every footstep, thought and
word spoken out of our mouths, and the decisions which we choose as
being constructive or destructive in our lives as well as those around us
for the good or the bad.

Because God is so great and so supreme being omnipotent,
omnificent, and omnipresent, having created every living being and
creature upon the face of the earth, He could equally instruct, guide,
and direct the very behaviors and/or speech of them that laid therein
which brings us to the life and a deed of Jonah.

Jonah was known as a prophet in Israel and generally, he was faithful
to the Lord in most of his actions, words, and deeds. It so happened one
day that he heard a word from the Lord instructing him to leave his
home and travel to Nineveh to alert the residents therein of their need

to seek repentance from the Lord because of all of their disobedience and wickedness as a people.

Probably, anyone who knew Jonah believed that he would be loyal to his task, and thus follow through with the command of the Lord in speaking to the people for he was such an obedient servant. But quite paradoxically, it seems that Jonah took the situation into his own hands feeling that the people were much too wicked and disobedient to be given such an opportunity to repent from their transgressions to the Lord and skipped the assignment.

Jonah therefore decides to catch a ship from Joppa so that he might travel on to the town of Tarshish instead, escaping the face of the Lord; thus, he immediately becomes disobedient to Him. Keep in mind that the Lord already knew that Jonah would make such a decision as He knows and is aware of all things at all times.

However, upon traveling upon the great sea, an equally great storm besets them and they are tumbled every which way to the point of probably being thrown overboard and cast into the sea. The seamen go to fetch Jonah who is sleeping below. After he awakens, they decide to cast lots or possibly roll dice to determine who brought this storm aboard. It turned out that Jonah was pointed out and out of pure fear, he admitted his disobedience to the Lord and now feels the Lord must be punishing him.

Jonah did not want the sailors to suffer any longer, so he asked them to cast him off the boat instead. That is exactly what they did and immediately following, the winds and the waves stopped and the storm dissipated. I am sure that the men became less fearful in those moments despite any lasting concerns which they may have felt for Jonah now lost at sea.

Jonah is saved by the Lord after being swallowed by a great fish and spending three days and three nights in its belly, then praying and asking God for His forgiveness for not obeying God's initial command and message to deliver to the people of Nineveh. Following, God allows the great fish to vomit Jonah upon the dry land.

Jonah eventually changed course and followed God's commandment. Oftentimes, it takes situations in our own lives to happen because of our free will, which the Lord has given to us to see the light or truth within ourselves or others and finally become obedient and follow the will and messages of our Lord.

How many times have we heard but chosen to turn away from what we knew were words from God speaking the truth in a matter right at us? Possibly, you have been directed to act or do something according to God's will but like Jonah, decided to go your own way... no matter how off track the course you became, digging deeper and deeper into the muck? What rude awakening did you experience like Jonah which made you pray and repent in those moments?

Revelation: My we remember the Lord our God in all of our thoughts, actions, and deeds.

Endeavor: May we be willing to become prophets of God's truth in our witnessing to others.

Prayer: Help us to listen for God's message no matter the circumstances and when we have done all that we could... let go, trusting in Him for our salvation knowing that He is our saving grace forever and ever. Blessed be the Lord. Amen.

REDEMPTION THROUGH JESUS CHRIST

But if the wicked will turn from all his sins that he hath committed, and keep all my statues, and do that which is lawful and right, he shall surely live, he shall not die. All his transgressions that he hath committed, they shall not be mentioned unto him: in his righteousness that he hath done he shall live.

EZEKIEL 18:21-22

So, the story goes that one day while Bathsheba was on a roof bathing with her handmaidens, when who should appear but King David himself. He had been out just strolling around on the grounds when his eyes caught ahold of Bathsheba in the water. It seems that he was quite smitten with her rare beauty from that day on as he cherished the ground upon which she walked. It seems that nothing such as shame or disobedience to God had anything to do with this sin that overpowered King David to no end.

As a matter of fact, he began to fantasize so much about what it would be like if he could just be with her, so he sent his servants or guards to get her from her room that same night. It made no difference to King David that she was married to Uriah who was out on assignment fighting as a leader in the war. He just had to have her, making her his concubine while that night Bathsheba broke her marital bond and committed adultery.

It was not like she had had any regrets or misgivings as she freely came into King David's bed chambers. Sometime later, she noticed that she had no menstrual cycle and found out that she was with child. Certainly, it could not have been her husband's child as they had been physically separated for months with him fighting on the battlefield in the military. Actually, the truth would have been made clear to the people that Bathsheba had been unfaithful to Uriah. What would she do and how did King David feel about all of this drama at hand?

I wonder, did Bathsheba feel any remorse for what she had done? Also, both she and King David had to know that his servants or guards and other concubines may have gotten word as to what was happening between the two in the heat of the night. Also, if they could have turned away from their wickedness during the first seduction or before Bathsheba became pregnant with child and asked for forgiveness from God and her husband, then surely, everything would have been made all right in their redemption by Jesus Christ for their disobedience towards God.

King David does plot to have Uriah returned to his marital bed on several occasions, however Uriah pleads full allegiance to his military duties and refuses to abandon his comrades for the pleasure of his wife. Uriah defies King David and causes him to seemingly be celebrated as a great military leader and places him on the frontline with the military fleet backing him up. Readers, don't misinterpret too quickly as Uriah is left abandoned and thus dies in service. Following, Bathsheba and King David marry to then produce a son leaving one to ponder where was justice in all of this betrayal and disobedience to our Lord? Just how could redemption in Jesus Christ be sought, let alone found in Bathsheba and King David's lives now?

Possibly, they thought that their marriage alone would resolve the deceptions, chaos, murder, pregnancy, and anything else that came asunder under his reign as nothing they had done together had been entered into lawfully and right. Where does righteousness ever enter the picture in these particular scenarios? And how could either one of them ever be thought of as blameless in all of the messiness which prevailed? Someone had to pay a price in the end.

So, God did hold both Bathsheba and King David at fault for all of the evil, misgivings, treachery, and wickedness which had befallen them even more by sacrificing their son's life for their disobedience. I wonder what they both thought regarding the death of their son? Does it make you the reader ponder this being made a punishable crime by death for another death? Or, this being the one loss which made both Bathsheba and King David acknowledge was a result of their own sins thus saith the Lord?

According to the verses above, if they had both repented and come face to face with their own sins, could they have been forgiven all of their trespasses? Or was the death of Uriah the unforgivable sin here? I wonder, was Bathsheba a part of that trickery or was she perfectly innocent of the crime yet to be unveiled by King David's command? Was it ever revealed that King David was the father of their premature son rather than Uriah as may have been thought?

Revelation: Whatever happened to the relationship boy David (King David) who slew Goliath had with the Lord? Had total disobedience dominated now?

Endeavor: Allow us to come correct with the Lord so that we can find redemption through prayer, fasting, and righteous living according to Jesus Christ.

Prayer: Help us all to take a closer look into our daily actions and behaviors set before God that they might be pleasing and presentable to Him. Enable us discernment in our decision-making for what is Holy and just in our Father's name. Amen.

EXALTATION

(Excessively Intense Sense of Well-Being, Power or Importance)

BEAUTIFULLY MADE

"I will praise thee; for I am fearfully and wonderfully made: marvelous are thy works; and that my soul knoweth right well."

PSALM 139:14

Every life is worth living despite one's parents, home life and familial circumstances regarding how one was conceived. Whether through natural conception via marriage or a consensual relationship via in vitro fertilization, or other means... God has the final say in His creations. For the Bible states all embryos are, "fearfully and wonderfully made" by the mighty hand of God. This speaks to the amazing fortitude, extraordinary insight and glorified omnipresence and omnipotence God takes in forming and bringing forth His creations.

Through our testimonies of miracles to the unveiling power and dynamic beauty of childbirth, we become witnesses to the awesome greatness and deliverance of God through His Almighty hands. Invisible to the naked eye, God's spiritual presence is felt all throughout the entire fetal gestation and birthing process of the mother's contractions to her dilations; unto the inevitable delivery of the baby or babies from mother's womb. Live birth of any creature is a miracle... particularly of a human being.

God Himself has formed all the inward and outward parts swaddled in their mother's wombs. Praise be to God for all of His marvelous works in the human body to bear it beautifully made! For God Himself has ordained all life...great and small. Therefore, giving honor and praises to God Himself for the life He has breathed into me and every living creature, I thank Him daily for His magnificent works. Glory be to God as we praise our Father above.

Are we ready to give God the honor, glory and praise for His marvelous works which He has placed into each of His living creations? No one can call the birthing process anything less than a miracle by all accounts. Correct? We should know well what He has done for us and continues to do for us every day in our blessed lives. Therefore, we should exalt His name as we proclaim, "Thanks be to God!" He's got the whole world in His hands as our soul knows. Correct?

Revelation: Proclaiming that we are fearfully and wonderfully made by God's precious hands!

Endeavor: May we learn to exalt God for all of His mighty creations.

Prayer: Blessed be to our Heavenly Father above for all that He has done, will do and continues to perform in and for the lives of His children… both child and adult. Help us to praise His name in our daily lives. Amen.

MIXED BETRAYAL

When the morning was come, all the chief priests and elders
of the people took counsel against Him to death: and when
they had bound him, they led him away, and delivered him to
Pontius Pilate the governor. Then Judas, which had betrayeth
Him, when he saw that He was condemned, repented himself
and brought again the thirty pieces of silver to the chief
priests and elders. Saying, I have sinned in that I have
betrayed the innocent blood. And they said, What is that to
us? See thou to that. And he cast down the pieces of silver
in the temple, and departed, and went and hanged himself.

MATTHEW 27:1-5

Suddenly, the Spirit of the Lord quite possibly, touched the heart of
Judas opening his eyes to his rude awakening and allowing him to see
the mistake that he had made in his mixed betrayal of Jesus. While
during the Last Supper when everyone was eating, Jesus had revealed to
His disciples His upcoming betrayal from one sitting at the table. Judas
Iscariot had denied the soon-to-be betrayal to his friend and leader,
Jesus of Nazareth, asking if it would be him.

The chief priests and elders more or less, placed a bounty upon Jesus'
life and offered up the thirty pieces of silver to whomever would betray
Jesus and allow the authorities to bring Him before Pontius Pilate prior
to His impending death. It is fair to say that Judas had probably known
days if not even weeks before Jesus' demise as to what he would do for
the taste of silver…some money given amongst the betrayal.

Quite possibly, again Judas may have pondered the consequences of his actions of bringing Jesus in but not to the point of his betrayal resulting in Jesus' death. Then, again as a disciple of Jesus, his teachings and acts of morality from Jesus may have overcome Judas' thinking and effected his decision to give back the silver to the priests and elders for the bounty on Jesus' life.

In any event, something happened to Judas in which he experienced a moment or moments of repentance and came to realize the consequences of his actions asking God for His forgiveness and deliverance from evil. Again, he must not have felt truly forgiven and/or delivered for his part in the deception as he followed in hanging himself and thus, taking his own life as well.

All of this begs the following questions. "Did God in fact forgive Judas for his transgressions toward Jesus? Did Judas act in enough time prior to Jesus' death? Did God forgive him for taking the silver as bounty toward Jesus' death? Did Judas ask God why he would be the deceiver in this matter? Could Judas take back what had been brewing in his heart toward Jesus?"

How many times have we as a people or as individuals been equally guilty of being caught up in some form of betrayal in our relations to spouses, other family members or friends? Have we been able to muster up the courage to take responsibility for our actions? Asking God first off for forgiveness for our trespasses toward another or others? Or have we simply fallen victim to our trumped-up circumstances at the time to justify our demonic chaos and actions?

Revelation: We as Christians must forever be cognizant of our Savior whom we follow and what His allegiance means to us daily.

Endeavor: May we come to understand the stain that betrayal in itself can produce in our own lives, let alone the lives of others.

Prayer: Please help us Lord to become aware of the naysayers in our lives so that we may be able to discern our friends from our enemies in Your name. And also, may we forever look to others as associated with our love for You first. Amen.

KNIGHT IN SHINING ARMOR

So, David prevailed over the Philistine with a sling and with a
stone, and smote the Philistine, and slew him, but there was no
sword in the hand of David. Therefore, David ran and stood upon
the Philistine, and took his sword, and drew it out of the sheath
thereof, and slew him, and cut off his head therewith, and when
the Philistines saw their champion Goliath was dead, they fled.

I SAMUEL 17:50-51

David was but a kid, a young teen in the eyes of the Lord who acted as
the shepherd boy watching over the flocks of sheep when one day, he
heard the voice of God calling him to a different time and place in his
life unlike other youth his age. Let's face it, how many teenagers would
have given God the time of day. As a matter of fact, I could almost hear
David questioning the Lord for how and why He was bugging him…a
mere teen to perform whatever tasks were needed that day when he had
done the unthinkable.

So, let's venture back into I Samuel chapter 17 to get more
information as to how David became God's chosen one. It seems that
the Philistine and Israeli armies were gathered together and pitched by
different terrains and mountains with a valley between them. They of
course were separated by land marking their territories or domains of
warfare and habitation as each tried desperately to conquer the other.
But most importantly, the Philistines insulted God and felt that their
god was superior to all others.

The Philistines had a giant named Goliath who was six cubits (nine feet) and a span (nine inches) in height. He was their knight in shining armor as he stood at attention with the finest and strongest of brass and iron metal protections covering his body from all harm from his helmet on down to his feet and his spear. His demeanor and presence amongst the Philistines demanded respect almost fit for a king as he was their chosen Savior in wolves' clothing.

Goliath had challenged the Israelites to send an opponent to fight against him and kill him, thus they become their servants or the reverse would occur and they the Philistines become their servants of war. David's three older brothers were to fight Goliath but they grew so afraid in facing him that they backed down. David was supposed to be watching over their flock of sheep but felt that he should be present to fight Goliath for the Israelites as he must have heard from God.

David had presented himself before the knight in shining armor as well. Carrying just five stones, a sling, and wearing some heavy metals which he took off because he felt them too heavy and non-usable for the task at hand is what David presented in his offense against Goliath. He had thought that since he had slayed both a lion and a bear in his previous encounters with the Lord's help and direction, that it only surmised that he could equally slay the giant with his sling and a stone.

As a matter of fact, this is what he presented to King Saul in his defense that he could kill the giant, Goliath as well. The king finally gave his blessing probably somewhat reluctantly at first, but feeling that what David had stated was evidence enough of his abilities to slay Goliath and thus, overcome the Philistines. So, off David went with the Israelite army at his side and he being open to the word of God in directing his footsteps.

Once seeing Goliath, he ran towards him with the five stones in his pouch and slingshot in hand. Then, David did the unthinkable. Taking out a stone he fixed it tightly in his sling and shot straight into an opening within Goliath's helmet. Obviously, this was an area in which the Philistines gave no thought as far as it being a weakness in his body armor. Down the great giant fell, shaking the earth. Immediately, David who did not bear a sword in a sheath, took Goliath's sword out from his sheath and cut his head off while he stood on top of him as his army ran away watching his demise.

Following, he went and presented Goliath's head to King Saul. Now, the Philistine army became the Israelite army's servants and they ruled in their areas. Certainly, this story presents itself as a parable minus character names to the readers. Never to think petty upon one's own abilities when the Lord is empowering you with the skills, knowledge, hindsight, experiences, and genius to complete a task at hand. How often do we forget to give the Lord thanks for how He empowers and exalts us by setting the course for our lives in handling even the smallest of tasks?

Maybe, our tasks are not so great as David's to accomplish, however, the mission may be as defining. Step to it and go to complete the assignment at hand. Many times, we may even hear a faint or strong voice coordinating us during the process but fail to acknowledge the Almighty God in our task. Let's keep in mind that God exalted David before King Saul even believed in his miraculous powers, courage, and honor in slaying Goliath. King Saul later became convinced to realize whose hands David was in and listened to that still, deliberate, voice to let the boy complete his task at hand.

Can you ever think upon a time when you heard the Lord directing your footsteps? How did that make you feel? Were you obedient or disobedient in willing to let Him have His will or did you do your will? Do you remember a time in which you felt exalted in a word or deed? How did that make you feel and did you remember to give thanks to our Father in Heaven for what He had done either in your life or someone you cared about?

Revelation: We can do all things through Christ Jesus who empowers us.

Endeavor: Keep us forever mindful of God's glory in our decisions and actions no matter our ages as we serve Him.

Prayer: May we become open to exaltation from the Lord as we watch, wait, and listen upon Him as He directs our steps. Also, may we humble ourselves before the Lord as I am sure David did many times especially as a shepherd of God's sheep and no matter what the task is set before us. Amen.

SURELY READY

Wherefore God also hath highly exalted him, and given Him a name which is above every name: That at the name of Jesus every knee should bow, of things in heaven, and things in earth, and things under the earth; and that every tongue should confess that Jesus Christ is Lord, to the glory of God the Father.

PHILIPPIANS 2:9-11

What a moment in the Spirit of our Heavenly Father, to know that soon and very soon He would witness the conception of His baby Son, Jesus Christ by a virgin named Mary after the Holy Spirit overpowered her with His omnipotence and omnipresence.

Most couples who want to conceive and make such efforts to do so are sometimes frantically overwhelmed in the process, but I'm sure that God was totally calm and just awaiting the moment that He knew the conception would happen. To watch over Mary and hope that she remained healthy enough, eating her vegetables and fruits and drinking and eating the proper dairy products, but watching her portions of meat and fat in her diet.

Possibly, once He may have flinched but knowing that He was all powerful and knew all things at all times… probably calmed His Spirit as He was surely ready to be a father. Certainly, He was blessed to have the Holy Spirit at His beck and call if He ever needed consolation, especially during Mary's labor and Jesus' birth. And my helpmate reflected that as "God jumped with joy, the angels in heaven were dancing!"

I cannot imagine what was happening in the high heavens after Jesus was born. God was probably like most fathers... a little excited and manning up to His creation of His son, Jesus. Naming Him such a name which was above every name under the sun. An eternal part of the Trinity of God the Father, the Holy Spirit, and now His Son, Jesus.

For humanity to bow before the name of Jesus of things in heaven, earth and under the earth was miraculous! What a Savior to be born for you and me to die on that cross to save us from our sins, transgressions, and trespasses was above reproach.

We cannot praise Jesus enough and give His Father the glory as Jesus was so highly exalted above all manner of man on earth. To know that Jesus was crucified, died, and arose three days later walking on earth amongst man before joining His Father, our Lord and the Holy Trinity can leave one speechless by such power.

And also, to know that it just wasn't the disciples and apostles of Jesus' time who walked with Him on the earth healing the sick, blind, lame and disenfranchised, but equally us today as we are disciples of Jesus working to gather the sheep and bring them home unto Christ. This is a constant work in the making as we call upon His name and confess that He is Lord and glory be to His Father.

How often do we think about the most beautiful conception of Jesus Christ? I wonder how many fathers were as cool, calm, and collected as our Heavenly Father upon the birth of their child or children? Possibly, if more fathers knew of the story and strength of God, that would help them to reflect only on positive moments during the birthing process as they help their wives or significant partners give birth?

Revelation: May we stay alert and prayed up to witness to the great things which our Lord has done for us and our families and friends.

Endeavor: Allow us to always remember what Jesus has done for us in order to help others in their walk with Him.

Prayer: Enable us to be surely ready to call upon Jesus' name in our daily living and give Him praise for the gift of life as we witness His precious miracles...our babies as they are being born in our sight. Amen.

NOT MY WILL, LORD

A double-minded man is unstable in all of his ways.
Let the brother of low degree rejoice in that he is
exalted. But the rich, in that he is made low: because
as the flower of the grass he shall pass away.

JAMES 1: 8-10

Many of us try to live two lives. One of stability, fairness, and righteousness. The other on the Richter Scale of instability, unfairness, and unrighteousness. He says the rich will pass away as the flower of the grass. Why, because we need to decide, which side will we depend upon and which road will we ultimately travel? Have we forgotten who decides our will, our lives, our destinies? Maybe, we have forgotten Him, our Father in Christ in all of this?

The Bible speaks of a man being double-minded who is unstable in all of his ways. But not the man or woman of low degree. This possibly means one who is humbled, fair, and righteous in all of one's life dealings shall be exalted by the Lord. His or her life won't fade away being lost in education and degrees, and big houses and luxurious cars only. Or the stock markets and other financial ventures and gains.

But through faithfulness of God, the low person shall be exalted by God. Now the word exalted may seem rather pronounced and too high up or esteemed to even fathom its meaning. According to the Merriam Webster Dictionary, exalt means to raise in rank, power, or character or elevate by praise or glorification. Certainly, we frequently do this for others in this life. But what about God's glory? How often do we exalt one another for that kind of glory?

For all of my life I knew of a man named James who came from very humble beginnings. He was a good son, honest and fair. He was my father. His mother had contracted tuberculosis when she was thirty-two years old and soon died. He was left with a younger brother and they basically ran the streets, smoking cigarettes, and getting into scrums with thugs, so he took up boxing later as a teenager.

My father quit school in ninth grade and eventually, around 16 and 14, he and his brother left home and found themselves barely making it on the streets and surviving. But they found a way as he became involved with street boxing to take care of himself.

Soon after, my father fell in love and married my mother at age 17 although his original plans were to go into the Army. But because she became pregnant with child, he did what he thought was the honorable thing to do even then despite circumstances. He knew that she had been suffering with a health disorder but had no idea of the magnitude of it and married her anyway.

She suffered from a disease called Sickle Cell Anemia and little was known about it then in the early fifties on into the seventies living in rural areas. There was however, more research and work being done about care management and its treatments in the larger urban areas like Detroit and Chicago as it so affected many people of color... particularly Black Americans.

Throughout the following four years, sadly they suffered some atrocities including losing three babies in death. Many doctors associated Momma's disease with the tragedies. Still, Daddy tarried and carried on with being the man of the house and going to work daily while trying to support all of us (the three children who did live and his wife in our home). He always came through with food, clothing, and shelter for his family as a man of his word. Thank you, Jesus.

There were many days that my mother ailed from her disease and needed blood transfusions, additional iron, and general hospital care because of her bouts. He would donate his blood to the American Red Cross for discounts on receiving the blood transfusions for his wife. Also, he had to take care of the finances and schedules of his children making sure we went to school. Luckily, a neighbor would check on us and helped Momma out when we were in grade school walking us to and from school.

Through the years, our mother suffered, but so did our father in the things which she could not supply him with. I am not saying that my father was a saint because I would not be telling the truth. He had his faults and vices which us kids became very aware of from gambling and frequenting the local black-owned tavern and drinking beer and hard liquor on weekends to name a few. However, he always made sure that us kids and Momma were taken care of. We were his number one priority.

Certainly, there were times in which us kids were not necessarily happy with our means but we made a way and got jobs to help sustain our means. It was like there was God always helping us in making ways for us to survive another day's journey. For many years, Daddy had been out of church and then one day, he returned. It happened sometime after he almost experienced death from a stabbing to his head at the tavern.

He was happy singing in the men's choir and being a soloist for Christ Jesus. Soon after when Momma was on her deathbed, Daddy was asking… no, begging her for forgiveness and telling her how much he had loved her all of those years in which they were together. Tears just flowed down his face. He was truly mourning her soon-to-be loss. I'll never forget watching and listening to him talk, not just to Momma but to God. It was like he was telling the Lord, "Not My Will, Lord, but Yours Will be Done!"

He remarried and they had a baby. He gained a couple of stepchildren whom I always called my brother and sister from the moments in which I met them as I felt like we were blood siblings. He stayed in the church and despite going through a stroke, bouts of gout, and cancer through the years, my father forever gave honor to God. God in turn rewarded him, exalting him to glory in his life on this earth. And, to the best of his ability, Daddy took care of his second wife as well until she went home to glory.

He was taken care of by his children and loved above all other fathers for the love and dedication which he bestowed upon both of his families. I believe that when our father surrendered his heart to the Lord Jesus, God exalted him above the earth for us to see as we all rejoiced in his great victory. "Not my will, Lord, but Your will be done." He was active in the church and became an upright brother in Christ as "the angels kept watch over him" and which was one of his favorite songs that he sang.

Based on what my siblings witnessed because I couldn't and didn't get there in time before his departure from this earth, it seems that our father didn't seem to suffer much in his final days. He was simply a poor, hurt, and once lost son who came home to be with his Father in Heaven as he gave his soul to Christ...sins and all. And his funeral was greatly attended by many friends and family members as he was so beloved.

Think about it. He was nothing more than a young man off the streets when the whole marriage thing started and he was probably starved for attention, love, and understanding himself having been abused and losing a parent at such a young age. What more can we do but surrender our all in all to Christ to then be exalted richly amongst our family and friends within our communities in the end?

How many of us will be given the extension of life to make right our wrongs in life? How long will our Father in Heaven allow us to sow our seeds before we come and stand before Him? Will we come to know the phrase, "Not My Will, Lord?" God's forgiveness is so great. For all of the strains, fights, losses, and hard living which my father had to endure in his life, God rewarded him in exaltation from this life onto higher ground based on his faith and dedication.

Can we all say that we will make it to the other side of the mountain as a good and faithful steward? What will it take to be forgiven and exalted by God? Will we emerge as God's faithful servants able and ready to serve others on earth as we will God in Heaven? And can we say, "Not my will, Lord... but Thy will be done?"

Revelation: It is one thing if man or woman exalts you on earth, but a greater thing if God exalts you before man and woman.

Endeavor: Allow us to see our faults and ask for forgiveness in all things so that we might be glorified (exalted) according to Your name, our Father which art in Heaven.

Prayer: May we all come to realize the glory which God has afforded for all of His children. Also, may we remember others as we exalt them knowing that their living here on earth has not been in vain. Amen.

FORGET ME NOT

Humble yourselves therefore under the mighty hand of
God, that he may exalt you in due time. But the God
of all grace, who hath called us unto His eternal glory
by Christ Jesus, after that ye have suffered a while,
make you perfect, stablish, strengthen, settle you.

I PETER 5: 6, 10

Job was a devout follower of our Lord; steadfast, patient, obedient, loving, giving, and genuine in his relationship with God. Basically, anything that had been given to him, he gave thanks and praise to our Heavenly Father for all that he had received. As I am sure in any and all challenges which he might have experienced in his life prior to Satan purposely entering his life.

In summary, God had issued a challenge of a different sort to Satan to test God's son, Job. God let Satan know that anything which He placed before him would be accepted by His sweet soul, Job. As a matter of fact, God challenged Satan to the point of hurting, but not taking every drop of life that he could possibly squeeze out from the soul of Job without taking his life.

Therefore, as the story goes… Job was stretched beyond the bounds of what any man should have to suffer or undergo in his devotion to our Lord. Within Job's own realm of personal power over his children, home, cattle, sheep, oxen, camels, land, crops, and servants he was stripped of everything by Satan as his faithfulness and loyalty to God was tested beyond belief.

How could Job withstand his losses, his grief, his feelings of wretchedness and possible wrongdoing for all that he had acquired during his lifetime, but then suddenly lose one thing after another in his life's journey. Times were so bad that his own wife told him to curse God for all that she believed He had done to His faithful servant Job.

Even Job's three friends who traveled from afar after hearing all that had befallen Job came to see what Job seemed to be suffering from. They could not and did not want to give any glory to God in all of this mess and heartache of Job being seen right before their eyes. Why they even thought that Job did not even look like his former self and questioned his loyalty to God above as he had shaved his head and scraped his body with a potshard.

I believe that Job had heard from God in revelation to humble himself under the mighty hand of God that in due time, He might exalt him. Job knew that God would not just forget, leave him and forsake him to the wiles of the Devil because he had learned of God's goodness, mercy, and grace through all of the years of his prior living. So why would He forsake him now? No, this should certainly make him reflect back on his past to all that he had received from the Lord.

Eventually, God believes that Job has been tested enough and restores every loss three times more than what he had previously acquired because of Job's steadfast devotion to God. Job had most definitely suffered for a great while, became made perfect, established anew, strengthened, and settled again in the love of his life. He was most certainly a testimony to all those around him regarding the greatness and beauty of the Lord in spite of circumstances and became exalted in due time by them on earth as well.

Truly, God had anointed Job early in his life to then be able to withstand all of the fiery darts of Satan and to remain if not entertain… new converts into the kingdom of God for all who witnessed Job's losses and most importantly, his gains over the course of fighting and enduring all of his obstacles. They actually witnessed great exaltation on earth of their friend, neighbor, and partner Job possibly, never to be seen again in their lifetimes.

How many of us can actually say that if we had endured what Job endured…not want to curse the ground that we walked on and possibly, everything in it? How many could remember our Lord and stay focused on Him despite what Satan was doing all around us? Could we remember all that God had once given us, brought us through, and remain faithful in our devotion to Him despite our trials and tribulations? What might we think upon to restore our faith if it becomes lost amid our testing from Satan?

Revelation: May we all look around us for the ways in which God exalts others on earth as His will may be done.

Endeavor: Allow us to be beacons of hope to those who are lost in the world while they search for God on His promises.

Prayer: Help us Lord to endure and strengthen us in whatever trials and tribulations may come our way and might we remember and not forget Your greatness to restore our gifts and wealth in spite of our losses as we lean upon You. Amen.

THE SIMPLE LIFE

Fishing on the banks of the free-flowing Mississippi River

Eating hot, golden-fried catfish and chilled, mustard potato salad

Tasting mouth-watering morsels of home-baked cakes and
scoops of homemade vanilla ice cream in Central Park

Devouring slices of red-ripened watermelon
while spitting the seeds out

Watching the gala parades march triumphantly down Main Street

Looking up at the grand ole' lighthouse atop Cardiff Hill

Pondering what the fuss was over the remnants of Mark Twain

Sneaking around the haunted Rockcliffe Mansion on Hill Street

Laying on the ground wondrously gazing
at galaxies and counting stars

Viewing with amusement Ted Mack, Lassie,
Walt Disney and Bonanza on TV

Entertaining festive picnics and horseshoe games at family gatherings

Fanning one's self singing gospels in the church choir

Drinking tall glasses of icy-cold lemonade sitting on the front porch

Running through blades of green grass feeling fancy-free

Catching lightning bugs and counting who caught the most

Pulling off freshly picked red tomatoes from their garden vines

Feeling one with nature and at peace with self and God

All, vivid memories of childhood days gone by...
days of the simple life in Hannibal, Missouri

Written by Donna Collier Rickman

The Literary Department

Kellogg Community College

1988

FAITH

(Steadfast In affection or allegiance
to someone or something)

WAKE UP EVERYONE

And brought them out, and said, "Sirs, what must I do
to be saved? And they said, "Believe on the Lord Jesus
Christ, and thou shalt be saved, and thy house."

ACTS 16:30-31

And so, they came… Paul, Silas, and Timothy to Philippi in Macedonia after Paul had received a vision for them to come forth and preach the gospel of Jesus Christ to the people. They had encountered a peculiar woman there who was possessed with a spirit of divination; telling others their fortunes and bringing in quite a bit of money for her masters.

After several days, Paul had commanded the spirit to leave her and it did. This made her masters extremely unhappy because she could no longer make an income for them so they set out to encamp Paul and Silas in the marketplace surrounded by the rulers after leading them there.

In turn, the rulers brought them before the magistrates and told them how they were doing damage to the city and bringing all kinds of trouble by not acting as law-abiding citizens according to the Romans' customs.

Following, everyone riled up against Paul and Silas beating them senseless and placing many welts upon their bodies before imprisoning them in their jail cells and making the prison guard to keep careful watch over them.

Later toward midnight, Paul and Silas held devotion with prayer and songs to God as the prisoners listened in. Soon after, a gigantic earthquake shook the foundations of the jail cells with all doors opening and everyone being set free. Surely, one could hear someone saying, "Wake up, everyone, you are free to go now!"

But not one left. Sadly enough, the prison guard thought they'd all abandoned ship and he'd catch the blame being found incompetent on his job. Therefore, he believed that he should be held accountable and die for not keeping a steadfast watch as he was about to take his life.

Luckily, Paul interrupted the prison guard's actions saving his life by telling him none had left. Falling to his knees trembling before Paul and Silas, he asked them what could he do to be saved? And they said, "Believe on the Lord Jesus Christ, and thou shalt be saved," as well as his own house of family members and occupants.

Think about what had just transpired at the jail cell by the prisoners and guard. First, look at how Paul and Silas had been placed there with their graven faith. One could say that they heard from God as to where they should travel next and were able to reach the people or certain groups of them as disciples of Christ. Secondly, their presence helped to save every prisoner including the guard from danger during the earthquake.

How often do we lose sight of our faith? Even to the point of blaming ourselves for every fault which we have made? Do we actually afford the Lord His opportunity to direct our lives and in most cases, save us from our own transgressions? Or do we rail and flail in the process, falling short as we bank on our own divinations or predictions for success or failure?

Revelation: God can deliver us all from all afflictions and persecutions as we have faith in Him.

Endeavor: Wake up, everybody, to one's anointed heritage of salvation in Christ Jesus.

Prayer: Believe on Jesus Christ and be saved; then, witness the miracles! Allow God His opportunities to make us as vessels of His great works unto others as we abide in Him. And may He equip us to fulfill His promises to those in need. Amen.

HOW GREAT THOU ART

And behold, a woman, which was diseased with an issue
of blood twelve years, came behind him, and touched
the hem of his garment: For she said within herself,
if I may but touch his garment, I shall be whole.

ST. MATTHEW 9: 20-21

When Jesus was on earth, He and His disciples walked among the masses restoring life to deceased individuals, exorcising demons, healing the lame, lepers, and blind, and the woman with the issue of blood. She had not just been ailing with this a day, month, or year but for twelve full years.

With my having a professional background in reproductive health, I doubt that this woman suffered from any kind of cancer for over twelve years and survived. If she was suffering from cancer all of that time, that was a miracle in itself due to lack of modern medicine, surgical procedures, radiation and chemotherapy which is available today. Rather, she may have suffered from fibroid tumors which caused the continuous blood flow and clots, extreme menstrual cramping, bloating and other side effects experienced within her body.

For her to walk out on her faith believing in the Holy word, work, and power of Jesus' touch or presence as she just touched the hem of His garment speaks to the kind of faith which she had unto death. Who knows for how long she held out waiting for this opportunity to be in the presence of Jesus.

Possibly, the Holy Spirit intervened as a Comforter and told her that just a touch of His garment would make sufficient for her to be healed. In any event, she had probably heard about if not witnessed several of the great works and miracles which Jesus had performed and thought that if He could do those feats, then surely, He could stop her issue with blood that she had suffered from for twelve, long and arduous years? "How great Thou art!" she may have screamed.

Still, she took a chance that Jesus would avail Himself unto her. This mere woman in a crowd of hundreds or thousands of sufferers who hoped to be healed like her. Particularly, since He did not put His hands on her or see her touch His garment.

Obviously, something happened in that split-second moment between she and Jesus to the point of His healing her and making her whole. Jesus believes that it was her faith which saved her throughout all of those years and to that finality when they connected and her change came.

If she could exhibit this kind of omnipotent faith in the presence of Jesus, then what can we do as people to be more forthcoming and visibly open in our faith to others? How can we be more faithful in our walk with Jesus? Can we tell others how He has brought us forward in our daily walk with Him as we serve a living God? Or, better yet, can we share His blessings with others after bringing us through our crises, doubts, and fears?

Revelation: How great thou art that we are readers of Jesus' great miracles from yesterday and are witnesses today of them.

Endeavor: Know we that as miracle workers, can also share in the healing of others by our faith.

Prayer: May we believe that if Jesus could heal the woman with the issue of blood based on her faith, then he can certainly do the same for others. Please allow us to grow our faith bringing others to Christ Jesus based on our faith and His healings. Amen.

BE DONE WITH IT

*Submit yourselves therefore to God. Resist
the devil, and he will flee from you.*

JAMES 4:7

How many of you have absolutely had it on your jobs? Working with co-workers who are envious and frustrated in their positions in relationship to yours. Feeling that they are less valued as you on the job; thus, disposable to the powers or entities that lay therein. In turn, how they react is sometimes very intentional, hateful, sporadic, and possibly, boastful in finding blame or drawing attention away from themselves unto you as the villain or point of focus in the matter. Their goal, to hurt you exactly!

Sometimes lying and placing blame in the wrong directions can land you sitting right next to the devil if he hadn't entered your mind, body, and soul yet. Some things to be remindful of are: God is the head and not the tail. We have to keep centered and focused on His will and not our own whereby, we resist the devil and he has nothing more to do to us or direct at others from us anymore. Therefore, he flees because he knows that God is our helper, leader, and our fortress as we submit to Him in our time of trouble and not him.

We must remember that in all things and at all times, we are not alone and that God even sends a Comforter to help direct our steps when we are confused, lost, and angry if we but draw upon Him. We have to be done with it whatever the outcome might look like and resolve to let go and let God handle everything. Not pockets of the situation, but the whole piece with all of our shackles of blame and shame.

When we finally release to Him, oh what relief, joy, and peace we often find knowing that the devil has left us and we are left standing in our Heavenly Father's arms safe and free from the devil's snare. We must not forget that we have a choice in our life to serve our Father or the devil, but we cannot do both to be a faithful servant of God.

The problem lay therein when we think and therefore believe that we should be able to handle all circumstances, all problems and concerns big and small without God. We should look back at our behaviors and then ask ourselves, "Did we allow God, our Father in the picture of the whole puzzle or did we just settle on letting the cards fly as they may in their shuffle... this way and that way rather than play the game? Did it start to look like a maze and we got caught up in a closed ending time and time again with no chance of a way out rather than hook onto God's saving grace?"

Revelation: We must let go and let God direct our lives.

Endeavor: Look for serenity in knowing whom to serve and be done with it!

Prayer: Please teach us faithfulness despite any possible weariness in becoming Your obedient servants knowing that You are our great Teacher and blessed Redeemer in this work on earth to be done. Amen.

I'M ON MY WAY

The name of the Lord is a strong tower; the
righteous runneth into it, and is safe.

PROVERBS 18:10

When it all started, I am not exactly sure. However, I believe that both the physical and mental symptoms and scars of fibromyalgia began shortly after my physical assault and trauma at the high school in 2005 when I suffered contusions throughout my body. All I do remember is that shortly after, my body most suddenly became inflamed, literally heated and filled with piercing pains from the result of what seemed like needles pressing into my nerves, especially in my arms and down my back into my thighs. It would also result in my having digestive problems as well as suffering from anxiety and depression, which can result in abnormal levels of certain chemicals in the brain that signal pain.

According to symptoms associated with this dreaded disorder from the Mayo Clinic, I suffered from most of them from their checklist. "Fibro fog" which was most definitely apparent. It impaired my ability at times to focus, pay attention, and concentrate on mental tasks at hand generally in the evening. Certainly, fatigue set in most hurriedly and would warrant itself available throughout the day. It was definitely more present after a long day at teaching. I wondered had it not been for me drawing on the Lord's strength, I don't know where I would have been safe in all of it to the point of even keeping a job in spite of everything.

At several times during the day after classes dismissed, I would generally lie down on my bench in my classroom and just try and catch my breath or tolerate the radiating, widespread pain which my body would be experiencing at that time. Luckily, our school had a wonderful custodian who would look in on me and let me rest. I thanked and appreciated her love and concern more than words could ever say. If it not been for her, I am not sure how well I would have rebounded from my episodes during those days. Truly, God was present as a strong tower and attentive in my welfare and healthcare as I was safe in His arms off and on the job.

My trek away from the physical effects of fibromyalgia seemed to evolve from many directions. Changes in major medications, exercise walking almost daily especially during the summer months along with better eating patterns and weight loss. And of course, receiving mental health services for my trauma. Most importantly, I became closer in my relationship with the Lord. I prayed more often, attended Bible Study and read God's words with my husband. God was most definitely present and the head of my life, directing my every footpath as I was on my way to remission!

I too was transferred to other positions within my school district. Certainly, this resulted in distress not being secure in a working building for a while but after it happened, despite changes from teaching at both the high school and middle school grade levels, and then going back into an elementary education classroom... all of the changes were for the better. Most importantly, I worked with a genuinely concerned principal who was willing to take a risk and work with me to take and make the necessary changes and adjustments in curriculum and teaching. Words cannot say thank-you enough for her leadership and support in my life and career crediting me as a Master Teacher during my evaluation some six years later! I'm on my way to some normalcy.

How often do we look around our workplace and wonder where our fellow Christians are and what they stand for on the job? If you were placed in a role of leadership at your job, would you have faith in accepting the lead with the Lord as your guide and leader or opt out? Do you believe that you would be protected at your worksite as was I by the Lord? Can you count the times in which you needed the Lord's reassurances that all would be alright?

Revelation: Had it not been for God on my side, where would I have been in my life?

Endeavor: May we look to God to showcase His disciples on our jobs so that we might feel secure in their care.

Prayer: Heavenly Father, lead me, guide me, and help me to keep the faith to follow You all the days of my life as You are a strong tower in my life no matter what the present is currently showing me or dealing my hand.

CHARTING WATERS

And He arose, and rebuked the wind, and said unto
the sea, Peace be still. And the wind ceases, and there
was a great calm. And he said unto them, Why are
ye so fearful? How is it that ye have no faith?

ST. MARK 4: 39-40

Imagine being on a ship with Jesus. Would you believe from the beginning of your journey that all would go well and everything said and done would be productive? Remember, you've got Jesus aboard, no need to ever worry or fear anything as He would be charting the waters for our course. Possibly, because Jesus was out of sight, He then became out of mind for the many disciples and seamen present in and around the large ship in which they travelled.

Therefore, any and all teachings and miracles which Jesus had previously shared with His disciples may have become null and void during those crucial moments when the winds and the waves began to wash over the ship flooding the floor and its walls, leaving them nowhere to escape from the deadly storm which was raging. I'm sure that the sky seemed like it was falling from heaven, all gray and black amidst the backdrop of everything.

Inevitably uncertain as to how to proceed across the high waves and sporadic winds if not at all, several of the disciples ran to the lower part of the ship to find Jesus. There, they found Him as calm as a mustard seed sleeping on a pallet not once bothered by the gusting and overpowering winds and waves of the sea. Immediately, they awakened

Him and said, "Master, careth not that we perish?" Wondering if He understood the urgency of the disaster which surely awaited them all without His intervention, they kept stressing this in their words and actions to Jesus.

Jesus then voiced, "Peace be still." And everything gently, yet quickly changed right before the disciples' eyes and ears as they sensed and heard peace not constant commotion within their ship any longer. Jesus questioned and asked, "What disciples have I taught here that are so fearful and show no courage, fortitude, or most importantly, faith which did not manifest itself through such a trial that had been set before them all aboard ship?"

Throughout this whole adventure, the disciples feared and questioned the wonders of Jesus. Remember that they had walked with Him on the earth and helped to heal all manner of disease and ailment amongst the people, but this situation proved itself differently in the lives of disciples calling upon faith of a different kind involving their own lives being at stake. Is this what challenged their faith or made their need greater somehow to believe in Jesus' teachings?

When all was said and done by Jesus below ship, the disciples asked themselves, "What manner of man is this that even the wind and the sea obey Him?" Obviously, they thought that they had witnessed all the power and glory magnified by Jesus until this latest venture which hopefully, made them have even more faith in the power of our Lord. Also, it quickened their spirits to be more prophetic and healing to the masses of people whom they would encounter along their journeys, especially in the presence of Jesus.

Such an experience to witness! If any of you had been present, would you have thought nothing to fear with Jesus aboard or called upon the Spirit of the Lord to intervene? Think of the times upon which you have been present and witnessed miracles or suffered great fears? What did you do during and after such an occasion(s)? Today, can we think of Jesus in the same light as able to intervene in all situations to the glory of God?

Revelation: We need to be ready to welcome that door of faith no matter the outcome in whatever situation presents itself.

Endeavor: May we remember "Now faith is the substance of things hoped for, the evidence of things yet not seen." Hebrews 11:1.

Prayer: Help us Lord to remember Jesus and the power which He anointed unto His disciples then and now on earth. There are still disciples that walk our earth today showcasing miracles to others amongst them. Amen.

ABIDING FAITH

We are troubled on every side, yet not distressed; we are perplexed, but not in despair; persecuted, but not forsaken; cast down, but not destroyed.

II CORINTHIANS 4:8-9

It would seem to me that every individual who arises from one's slumber each morning, would have to get his or her praise on by falling down on one's knees and thanking their Maker, our Creator above. Because with every negative and or recurrent incident, or fiery dart thrown at us, such as a shooting, house foreclosure, divorce, alcohol or drug addiction, and so forth, that goes on in our daily living; how can we not say, "Thank You, Father, for another day's journey and I am so glad to be here because you bought me; yes, carried me through again!"

Having become troubled, perplexed, persecuted, and feeling cast down we know that depending upon God, we can do all things through Christ who strengthens us. We have abiding faith sanctioned through the hymns that we can make it despite or in spite of our struggles as we "Come this far by faith leaning on the Lord and trusting in his Holy word."

We therefore, triumph and feel non-distressed or in despair; not forsaken, and undestroyed. For we know that faith is the substance of things hoped for; the evidence of things yet not seen. And that despite all of Satan's tactics or plans to harbor harm, deceit, fear, and death; God will prevail manifesting His goodness, mercy, and grace to all those whose believe and seek His word and truth.

We must therefore, hold on and abide in God's faith no matter our circumstances and no matter how long the course. We must seek to hold fast to God's hand full of hope and everlasting life knowing that our time on this earth is but for a while, but our time with God is forever. There are things that we will go through but surely endure which will make our faith only stronger in our Heavenly Father if we believe in His word knowing He will never leave us.

Are there times in which we do feel perplexed on every side without a wing or a prayer to hold unto? Do we fall on our knees and thank our Heavenly Father for all that He has allowed us to do and prevail in? Have we been dependent upon God's word and obeying the Holy Spirit? Lest, we forget the sacrifice which God's Son, Jesus made upon the cross for you and I that we might have abundant life for today and tomorrow?

Revelation: There is everlasting hope in abiding faith.

Endeavor: That we seek our Heavenly Father earnestly each morning and abide in Him throughout our days.

Prayer: Help us Father to hold on to Your truth and know that You can make a way out of no way and provide refuge for us in our deliverance as we come this far by faith trusting in His Holy word. Amen.

OUR DOUGLASVILLE COMMUNITY

But continue thou in the things thou hast learned
and hast been assured of, knowing of whom thou hast
learned them; And that from a child thou hast known the
holy scriptures, which are able to make thee wise unto
salvation through faith which is in Christ Jesus.

II TIMOTHY 3:14-15

I can remember the beautiful and handsome, yet hard-working, happy-go-lucky and sometimes hardened or sad faces with jubilant or joking laughter from the neighbors within our black community called Douglasville. I can see them now, our elders, other adults, teens, and kids alike all gathered together for a neighborhood barbecue or picnic like a block party although, I don't remember anything of that size occurring. The only thing missing was when the carnival came to town or a parade was seen marching down Broadway in Hannibal, Missouri.

To name those families in Douglasville were as follows: us, the Collier's, Davis's, Smith's, Longmire's, Farris's, Mr. Pete, Mr. Paul, Miss Pinky, the Minor's, Frazier's, Lechers, Conley's, King's, Robert's, Green's, Haley's, Miss Susie, Miss Josephine, the Bright's, Tinsley's, Brown's, Simon's, Coleman's and The Eighth and Center Streets Baptist Church (a few streets over from Douglasville). Certainly, it took a village to raise a child then, when adults felt an allegiance to participate in most kids' upbringings as the parents would allow them.

Without the help of churches, I really don't know where our souls would have been. My siblings and I attended Sunday School and church services at Eighth and Center. We also attended summer camp at a Christian campsite without fail into our teen years. Luckily, we were able to attend Bible School held each summer for years held at the Mennonite Church and they provided us with food and Christian sustenance. Along with us kids singing in the youth choir, our mother acted as church clerk when she was able and not sick.

I cannot thank God enough for His tender blessings and sovereign, loving care. He placed people in our lives who were sanctioned and holy in God's eyes who shadowed over us in His loving righteousness and glory. Living in Christ, he saved our family time and time again in our life's journeys and roadblocks. He literally lifted us from poverty with the help of family and friends by giving us food to eat, putting clothes on our backs, and shoes on our feet from the jobs we kids were able to secure.

It was a time when, most anybody could be called upon to help a neighbor out with some chore or activity or borrow a cup of sugar or milk. And certainly, gardens were plentiful and growing as we exchanged prime vegetables of the day... carrots, tomatoes, peppers, cucumbers, and the like as Daddy and Momma grew tomato and grape vines in the backyard and collard greens in a side pocket of the front yard. Also, recipes were shared amongst the women who were wives and mothers. Likewise, they'd sometimes bring homemade jellies, banana bread, a cake, cookies or a pie by the house to share.

I can remember my mother hosting card parties amongst her friends who would come by and get their hair pressed with Momma's hot combs and then pay her a little something for her efforts. They'd have a good time up there smoking their cigarettes and winning at the latest deck of cards drawn in Spades or Black Jack and laying out the dominoes.

Generally, these women including my mother would be getting the latest scoops regarding Douglasville news or other predominantly black communities in town. Sometimes, it would be about who was seeing who...dating or who was pregnant again with their third or fourth child, and so forth. There was nigh a quiet mouth in the room because it seemed everyone had some comments to contribute to the conversations. There was lots of gossip… some which I cannot share, that's for sure.

My mother suffered from Sickle Cell Anemia, a blood disease really unknown amongst the African American community back in the 60s and early 70s and she would come down with bouts of pain in her crises. Usually, two or three neighbors would always come by and attend to her and us kids when they could. Plus, on occasion, would send some meals or sandwiches our way.

Special thanks to whom I called Momma's sisters and or mothers… Mrs. Claudine, Mrs. Ruth, Mrs. Johnnie Elsie and Cousin Pauline Blackwell who would help us with Momma and or chores and meals to feed our family. My brother, sister and I can't say thank you enough to these women who are no longer living for their dedication in time, talents, love, and care to our family in our times of need. Truly, they were God's merciful angels on earth.

Each one of the families and our church provided some sort of nurturance and care-giving skills, knowledge, wisdom, truth, God's saving grace and validation to be a young, black woman growing up in my hometown. Along the way, we learned to survive our family's poverty, Mother's illness, and Father's weekend drinking binges. With so many social, physical, and economic problems that challenged our modes for life, liberty, and the pursuit of happiness in everyday living, God held us tight and kept us in our family's home.

As the scripture above states, we kids learned early in life about the holy scriptures which helped us to understand salvation through faith in Christ Jesus. Through our times in attending Sunday School and going through baptism and other Christian rituals, we came to know God's truth for our lives and have served Him throughout our years of living. I have certainly learned that all is given by inspiration from God.

What then can I say, saved us from the wiles of this world? The determination, spirit, and fight which we witnessed in our parents' lives. And our will to overcome, triumph and not be defeated but hold on to God's promises of great blessings, along with the goodness of the Douglasville community are memories we shall cherish always!

How often do you as the reader praise God for the goodness of the people within your communities while growing up? Is it fair for me the writer to ask such a question in light of all of the violence occurring within communities today whether urban, suburban or rural? Do you find yourself yearning for anything that I have written regarding the love, care, and sharing shown with living in a close-knit community? Have you found a church which you can congregate at and feel a sense of family for your children to experience as well?

Revelation: Let us rejoice in what the Lord has given us in our youth, family, friends, a Christian church and Christ Jesus.

Endeavor: May we become wise in salvation through faith in Christ Jesus.

Prayer: Help us Lord to remain mindful of You and all of Your abundance, salvation, and glory keeping the stories and memories learned in our childhood and teenage years abreast in our lives and families today to thus share the love through our descendants. Amen.

FORGIVENESS

(to cease feeling resentment
toward an offender)

TENDER CARE ALWAYS

"And be kind to one another, tenderhearted, forgiving one another, just as God in Christ also forgave you."

EPHESIANS 4:32 (NKJV)

There are so many kinds of domestic violence, and abuses being committed throughout the world today. Having experienced both verbal and physical trauma in my teenage years as well as adulthood would qualify me as a justifiable victim of abuse. Or at least it would seem so considering everything which I had endured and am still fighting to overcome.

Prone to non-forgiveness, what seemingly raised its ugly head was conditionally directed anger from my physical and mental traumas, resulting in what I thought were justifiable ways of living; nightmares, tremors, agitation, and fear. However, all of these conditions actually became self-perpetuating, both acute and chronic leading to my being identified as an undeniable victim too many times over.

Levels of trauma had been so great that I had to seek counseling for both outpatient and inpatient hospital treatment for diagnoses of Post-Traumatic Stress Disorder (PTSD), severe anxiety, and clinical depression. This fortunately enabled me to confront issues of self-inflicted shame, self-denial, rejection, low self-esteem, major anxiety and enraged anger found in abuse.

Learning to forgive my abusers became a major obstacle for me to overcome in my recoveries. I had to learn that it was not only my abuse to myself to let others hurt me, but that I was a child of God. I sincerely believed that through Jesus Christ who died on the cross for my sins, that I could begin to forgive my abusers. However, I still have problems forgetting the incidences and attend outpatient therapy and group counseling to help cope. One main difference, though, is that I speak out today about my past abuses and that has certainly helped in my healing process.

Hope at once became like an enemy to me to believe that I would put the title of "victim" behind me for good. It happened far too often and consumed my very being for too many years. How could I escape its overly powerful jaws, demeanor and strife? And to become kind and tenderhearted meant what, and to whom in forgiveness? Why did I have to forgive my abusers for their sins? After all, they caused me indescribable pain, suffering, and sorrow deep down in my heart.

I had to go back home in learned teachings and time to remember the love of my parents and the caregiving which I gave to my mother from age nine until my late teens after high school and the care given to me by neighbors, family, and church family to even exist. And more importantly, I had to remember Jesus hanging on the cross and all that He had endured to ask God to forgive His persecutors who nailed Him to the cross where He bled and died for their sins and ours.

I now answer the question, "Has God softened my heart toward everyone and everything I negatively encountered in my life during those periods of disarray and disillusionment?" I can honestly say, "Yes!" I also have a different attitude regarding the word "victim" and all that it entails. It might come but it must go so that we can be delivered in our purpose here on earth. Let go and let God prevail so that we can press onward to His victory and our victories of overcoming as well!

Have you asked God to help you in your life's journey and/or tribulations? Grace and mercy to remove the hurt, bitterness, and ugliness to then strengthen and forgive you as well for any transgressions harbored against another? Also, help in asking for hope and a future to recognize your own faults and step up to your own responsibilities as a dignified human being? And most importantly, the willingness to share the forgiveness of the Lord in, with, and for others in your past sufferings and or mistakes?

Revelation: Stay resolute to overcome life's challenges no matter how grave the consequences to ourselves.

Endeavor: Remember, one's hope is built in Jesus Christ and upon His forgiveness of our sins as we take up our own crosses which we bear.

Prayer: Help us Jesus to become resilient and productive in my recoveries and always spiritually knowledgeable in Your tender mercies. Likewise, help us to become true disciples of Yours towards our fellow man in discernment of character and life choices for our betterment and others. Amen.

BLISTERING FRILLS

With all lowliness and meekness, with long suffering,
forbearing one another in love, endeavoring to keep
the unity of the spirit in the bond of peace

EPHESIANS 4: 2, 3

And in the heat of humanity's pouring rain… small wind gusts began to form, sharpen, and blow amongst the fray of the morning dew in many cities across America as people cried out and screamed, "Black Lives Matter!" and "I Can't Breathe!"

Races had been kind and understanding, lowly and meek marchers withstanding long suffering, forbearing one another in love, sympathetic to the needs and concerns of the greater movement. There had been some accounts of looting by out of towners. No specific group of protestors held any angst against another. They marched as one united front forgiving and loving one another as God's children in the plight at hand, keeping the unity of the spirit in the bond of peace.

More specifically, George Floyd age 46, was killed by four police officers just days before. One officer had acted as the lookout, while two of them held his body down on the street as the fourth had forcibly pinned his knee directly into George's neck for almost nine minutes as he laid on the street dying from asphyxiation.

Recently, tensions had been building amongst the police departments and growing protests of black, white, Latino, Native American and other ethnicities of people within urban, suburban, and rural communities.

National and international protests were occurring over the plight of African Americans dying needlessly at the hands of police officers. George's death was the pinnacle at the heart of this matter of injustices seen and unseen across the country.

What was simply meant as frills on an afternoon in Minneapolis, Minnesota; to those four police officers in the heat of that blistering June day became known as a death warrant to George. Bystanders were present and witnessed such an atrocity as they pleaded for George's life. A young twelve-year old girl witnessed the whole account while videotaping George crying out on several occasions that he could not breathe and calling for his mother while he lay dying right in front of America on live television.

It was as if the Holy Spirit was leading and directing the protests as people rallied together uniting and proclaiming the truth of God that laid before them. The majority acted as apostles and disciples doing the work of the Lord in this great movement. Outside of prayer, what more was there to do and be stated. God was pleased with the work of His children during most of those days!

How often do we as Americans just compartmentalize a scenario which we witness and jump to mere assumptions rather than looking at the facts for what we know are true? Can one say that the public situation witnessed regarding the death of George Floyd was just hearsay to the naked eye? Can we as a body of Christians join in movements which we know are of God and His plans of truth, justice, and prosperity for our lives? Could you reading this essay have seen yourself marching along with the protestors during those heat-filled days for a greater cause in the Lord?

Revelation: We are all our brother's and sister's keepers in spite of others' blistering frills.

Endeavor: Enable us to continue as Your apostles and disciples here on earth despite the negativity and strife set before us by our opponents.

Prayer: Help us to put the golden rule in action for our treatment toward one other. Also, that we may forever remember Jesus' teachings as He went out and healed the sick, the lame, and lepers in their colonies along His footpaths shining as a beacon of light for all who travelled His way. In turn, they carried His light forth as did the marchers or protesters searching for God's truth. Amen.

SAVE IT FOR ANOTHER DAY

Likewise, ye younger, submit yourselves unto the elder. Yea, all of you be subject one to another, and be clothed with humility: for God resisteth the proud, and giveth grace to the humble.

I PETER 5:5

And it is written in St. Luke 15: 11-32 that a man had two sons. The younger had asked his father for his share of the bounty that was due him from his inheritance. So, his father splits up his share and gives it to him. Shortly after, the young man takes all of his riches, belongings and sojourns to a faraway country.

Therein, he acts derelict, squandering his money, lying with women of the night in the most luxurious of accommodating inns, buying the richest of textiles and clothing around, eating the fattest of calves and extravagant meals, and drinking the hardest spirits available.

Due to a famine in the land, he ends up losing all that he had accumulated and goes to work feeding the swine and eating their slop. I am sure that at that time he had reflections back home to the good life which he had been living with his father and older brother. When and where had he gone wrong?

I'm sure that thoughts of what he had done with his life seemed almost too hideous to bear. Thinking upon the servants working in his father's house, he surmised that they had been much more secure than he had ever been on his own and were certainly cared for, had good food to eat and were sheltered.

Thoughts of disrespect toward God, the Father and his own

biological father began to tear him apart to the point of his being regretful, fearful, and full of blame and shame for his actions. Truly, he had not left his father's home representing all of the values and morals which he had been raised up in and had failed to submit himself unto those principles once out in the real world on his own.

He became so humbled that he had to go back home and ask his father as well as the Lord for forgiveness for all of his juvenile behavior. Upon his homecoming, his father spotted him afar off and ran to greet him as he had actually mourned his absence in witnessing his lost son's return home.

All of the best adornments, foods, clothing and riches were splurged over his reemergence in the household by his father. His brother was distraught over all of the misplaced allegiance by their father to his younger brother. All that his father could say was that his lost son had come back home now.

Nothing else had mattered. God had given grace to him by bringing him home safely. He was dead but now is alive; lost but now was found said his father. Therefore, his son was forgiven for all of his juvenile misbehaviors, worry, and disrespect and was basically told to save it for another day!

Just how often in our childhood, had we become remorseful and asked our Father in heaven for forgiveness for our transgressions toward our elders? Did any of you ever go away like the younger brother, lose all that you had, then ask for forgiveness from your parents? If so, have you thought about the lessons learned through all of it that we may pass them down to our children and our children's children through the generations?

Revelation: May we remember to be obedient toward our parents.

Endeavor: Remain humble toward others that we may find grace in the Lord.

Prayer: Help us to be respectful, yet submissive to our elders in our walk on this earth. Let us remember their teachings and relationships with our Lord so that when we grow old and weary, may be afforded the same respect, loyalty, and love from our grandchildren. Amen.

SIMPLY SPEAKING

And the apostles said unto the Lord, Increase our faith. And the Lord said, If ye had faith as a grain of mustard seed, ye might say unto this sycamine tree, Be thou plucked by the root, and be thou planted in the sea; and it should obey you.

LUKE 17:5-6

Faith has been written and described as the substance of things which we hope for, but the evidence is yet not seen. In our everyday life, how often do we have faith that we will wake up the next morning, wake up our families to eat breakfast which we cooked, be ready to go to work and school to learn and grow, and then return safely home as if that should be the way things go.

However, between our working days on into the evening and early morning hours, we have lost loved ones, our homes, vehicles, and jobs to Covid 19 which were not the pictures of the evidence of living for which we had seen. So, does that make our faith any less that such calamity of such an enormous nature should befall our country, and even the whole world as a pandemic?

Can you imagine the Lord talking to you as He did the apostles who asked for ways to increase their faith? Simply speaking, the Lord told them what would be required. Having the faith of a mustard seed by telling a sycamine tree or a sycamore tree, which is known as enormously grand and lush, to move and be planted in the sea and it should obey you.

Literally speaking, the above verse seems almost distant and non-relevant in times like these, granted more lives have been saved than not and people have survived the imminent crisis and prevailed amongst the living. But to have the faith as a grain of mustard seed, and for it to obey our heeding is such a tall order to be filled for much of mankind.

There are those essential, front-line workers who put themselves in such a category of faith believing that they are doing their jobs as God commanded to help the sick and shut-in from their grief and illnesses. Thus, allow them to safely return home to their families without any hurt or harm from the contraction of the Covid 19 virus.

Basically, the Lord is saying, you do your part and I will do the rest. Just how many of us truly believe that? And I wonder, how many apostles were in step with the words which our Lord spoke to them that day about how they could grow in faith. In what ways did they challenge their Father or obey His words?

How often do we as Christians challenge our faith? Do we place our faith in the Lord's hands or do we simply just act upon it in our own ways? Are we reading the scriptures daily to find ways in which to increase our faith as well, as did the people in the Bible amidst their various situations and travails?

Revelation: Know that the Bible allows us to find instances of faith in action throughout.

Endeavor: May we seek to envision in our lives that which is not yet seen by our walk with the Lord.

Prayer: Remind us, Lord, in our daily lives and pursuits, that we walk by faith and not by sight. Most importantly, that You order our steps in whom, what, why, and where we walk daily in Your light. Amen.

FREEDOM

(The Quality or State of Being Free
or Absence of Necessity, Coercion, or
Constraints in Choice or Actions)

FEATHERS OF A BIRD

Stand fast therefore in the liberty wherewith
Christ hath made us free, and be not entangled
again with the yoke of bondage.

GALATIANS 5:1

I have come to learn about justifiable liberty as having one's freedom to be and act as the feathers of a bird that freely (without hesitation or bondage), fly, glide, and strut through the air and all about from one destination or perch to the next. Birds are blessed with the closeness of their feathers to move easily through and exist in sometimes adverse weather conditions with the greatest of ease if they didn't fly to warmer climates and regions for survival. But just think of all the species of birds which God has made and think upon the many listed in the Bible.

It is obvious that God took an examination and determined the gravity to which man and other species within the universe evolved and functioned amongst the life and activity of a bird. One could also deduce that God believed this creature to be the most agile, skilled, productive, and protective in the universe short of the wings of angels in flight and their service as messengers of God. Most certainly, there is a beauty and majesty among birds from the smallest such as a hummingbird or dove to the largest, an eagle or condor with its magnificent wing span and armored protection.

It is stated in our Bill of Rights of the Constitution regarding man's and woman's rights to pursue justice and fairness in all matters that relate to his or her rights under the law having life, liberty, and the pursuit of happiness high on their agenda of opportunities to explore and live out in America. Granted, not all Americans believe they have these rights as attested to in our United States based on the impoverished populations seen throughout the nation.

Just as Christ hath sanctioned us as free and able, willing vessels to submit to His words, omnipresence, and power; so do we have the ability of not becoming entangled with the yoke of bondage which can encompass so many things. Drug and alcohol addiction, human bondage such as slavery and human trafficking, and physical and mental abuses to name a few are infusing our country with so much strife and indifference felt and witnessed among the people.

Before Jesus died on the cross, was buried, arisen and sent up to sit at the right hand of God, He walked amongst the people and could sense their pain, hunger, thirst, needs, disenfranchisement and so forth through touching and feeling their essence or being in close proximity to their ails at the exact moment He encountered their presence such as the woman with the issue of blood. Why? Because He was blessed by God His Father to suffer such, yet always recover for the next outreach in His destiny on earth. Jesus was by example, the Great Teacher of disciples and apostles and man scripturally in the Bible, proclaiming God's word.

We need to be reminded of the feathers of a bird which we have to exist in liberty and freedom. Not held to anyone's norms of bondage or otherwise, self-imposed against our person. We have a right to liberty. How many times have we lost our liberty to self-imposed forms of bondage? Do we remember to call upon Jesus to help release us from our states of bondage to live freely? Do you ever feel God's protective wing around you in your daily struggles, thus allowing us room to release our freedoms and exist in liberty according to our rights under the law?

Revelation: Look around and assess your liberty. Is it up to par in your daily living or do you need to make some repairs and step it up a bit with God's help?

Endeavor: Live a life exemplary of what God has given all of us despite the often long odds and pitfalls in today's society.

Prayer: Ask God to help us remember the feathers of a bird and the purpose and power for which they possess and liberate us thus, helping us to avoid bondages not of our liking or lifestyles accordingly. Amen.

PROSPERITY, NOT SHAME IN THE LORD

For I know the thoughts that I think toward you, saith the Lord, thoughts of peace, and not of evil, to give you an expected end.

JEREMIAH 29:11 (NKJV)

Jeremiah was a prophet who sent a letter to the elders, priests, prophets, and people who became captive and carried away from Jerusalem into Babylon by Nebuchadnezzar. The Lord had let them know that they should not be falsely misled by false prophets and diviners who prophesied in the Lord's name, since He had not sent them. He would welcome evil upon those who chose for His people to be misled and lose hope.

God knew the plans for His people. He didn't want them to be harmed but wanted them to prosper giving them hope and a future for an expected end even some seventy years later. Jeremiah was giving them the truth of his words as they came directly from the Lord. The Lord wanted His people to have peace on earth and not to worry needlessly about life in general.

After being placed in captivity, God wanted them to build and live in houses, plant gardens and eat the ripe fruits of them, multiply and bear children, both daughters and sons, and increase in number. They were God's children and no way was He going to send them out without proper clothing, shelter, and food harvests to survive.

Many times, in our daily lives, we have probably asked the questions, "Who am I, what is my purpose in life? How do I get there? How long will it take? What resources do I have to help me? Who will I trust to help me get there in reaching my goals?"

First and foremost, we must put the naysayers and the haters behind us as we rely upon the promises of the Lord. Relying upon the power and guided direction of our steps from our Father is the exact way to go even if it means becoming captive in our hopes and futures separated from those we'd hope would be supporting us.

Family and friends may not see our visions and future that God is taking us to. There may be too many hills, valleys, and obstacles with little or no visible peaks which others can see. So, they believe falsely; not upon the promises of the Lord and work of Jeremiah. Oftentimes, they may even try and talk us out of our plans and futures during such aha moments which is the work of the devil.

During times like these, we need to hold on to our Savior and remember that God has not left us in despair, heartache, and pure evilness surrounding our journey. How often have you felt abandoned and left with little to no hope in your daily life? Do we let the world and all of its drudgery take us out of the ballfield of hits? Or have we listened for the direction which God is leading us in to go to score a home run?

Revelation: Know that our Father loves us and wants only peace for us in all that we do.

Endeavor: May we all find prosperity and not shame in the Lord, with a hope and future.

Prayer: Help us to hold fast to Your place of freedom in our lives, Lord, as we blossom inward and outward standing in Your word. Please allow us to become free from shackles which have proven to be confining and injurious to our bodies, minds, and souls as You free us from all known and unknown harm. Amen.

RUN THE RACE

But in all things approving ourselves as the minsters of God,
in much patience, in afflictions, in necessities, in distresses, In
stripes, in imprisonments, in tumults, in labors, in watchings,
in fastings; by pureness, by knowledge, by longsuffering,
by kindness, by the Holy Ghost, by love unfeigned.

II CORINTHIANS 6:4-6

In comparing the jail time experiences which Nelson Mandela had at Robben Island Prison versus Paul in Philippi, both had become imprisoned because of the choices which they had made in their lives as directed by a higher power. The main decision being to follow God and share the genuine goodness found therein for salvation from Jesus Christ and the tasks which they were selected to perform while living on earth. They had in many ways become ministers of God's words having suffered through afflictions, being in distress, going through their imprisonments and beatings, following through with their labors possibly by fasting.

Paul had been named Saul previously at birth and had been a known persecutor of Christians, jailing them sometimes to their execution in his adulthood. Through a change in his life, God knocked him off his horse and there was a flash of light and he became blinded. Then he heard Jesus' voice ask him, "Why persecute me?" He was given the name Paul shortly afterwards with his vision restored and anointed by God to be an apostle. One to bring the message of God to the people.

In that anointing, he would sojourn the countryside and provinces healing and restoring the sick, the lame, and the blind many times with other apostles and friends such as Silas and Timothy. On one occasion, the governing powers of Rome had had it with all of the showmanship and outright healing that they had heard and seen was taking place in the city of Philippi. So, they gathered together and decided to make some changes concerning what Paul was doing.

They thought that he had become a distraction to the Roman people most certainly aligning him with the teachings of Christ. Such officials probably believed that the people were looking upon Paul like a god to be worshipped and idolized. They literally witnessed and again heard the many miracles in people's lives which had been restored because of Paul. So, the governing powers decided that swift action needed to happen most immediately.

They had him beaten, arrested and put him into prison with Silas. Soon if not within days, Paul must have received an awakening from the Lord, God Himself and wrote a letter to his church in Philippi informing them of his fate. God had surely now given him the time, abilities, and wherewithal to surmise what should happen in all of this up to his release. Through it all, Paul remained steadfast, hopeful, decisive, and strong in his belief and faith in Jesus Christ and His teachings and did not tarry.

On the other hand, the world has embraced the faith, boldness, wisdom, empathy and loving spirit of Nelson Mandela named at birth as Rolihlahla, one of the greatest fighters for freedom of all time! His unselfish loyalty to do what was right toward Apartheid in South Africa and his giving spirit to help others during his lifetime in his country, family, and the world is his legacy to us.

In his letters from prison, he mostly wrote to his family, in particular a daughter telling and entrusting them to never lose hope that he would be released and able to rejoin his family and the movement back home. However, through all of his years of imprisonment, he never lost faith in God and would seek Him out for many of the decisions which he made regarding his fight against Apartheid with fellow fighters and militants back home. Nelson was one who would not necessarily speak God's name publicly as he wanted everyone to decide for him or herself whom to worship and follow spiritually even though he would honor God daily.

As we witness the impact of Mr. Mandela's life, may it ignite a fervor in us all... to stand up for justice, human rights, decency and dignity; voice and write our concerns in pen; and become involved within our communities, cities and countries helping others who are less fortunate than ourselves to rise up and overcome societal racism and disenfranchisement to become free! Overall, that was his first and most important task and responsibility to his country.

After all, Mr. Mandela was imprisoned for life in 1964 even though he did not serve all of his years and was released early many years later, he became a dual recipient of The Nobel Peace Prize for Freedom. Blessings, and may we continue our fight for everyone's freedom across the world, passing on our torches of compassion to others down through the generations for both the sake and well-doing of Paul and Nelson as they had run the race in each man's perspective journey as directed by God. To have been as elevated and exalted by God Himself in the lives of both of these men must have been some marvelous revelation to witness!

That they both sought God in all of their ventures and footpaths was truly something to revere. When have we ever felt the hand of God elevating us from our present state to a different state to do His work according to His will and remained obedient throughout? Can we really imagine the fortitude it took for these servants of God to remain hopeful, yet productive in their assignments on earth? Do we really have an understanding as to why these two servants persevered in their duties to man as they did despite or against all odds?

Revelation: Let us continue to accept the call for which God has placed upon our lives no matter the doubts and obstacles in running our life's races.

Endeavor: Throughout our imprisonments, both mental and physical, may we remember You who holds the power of our release to freedom.

Prayer: Allow us, Lord, to travel the paths which You have for us to do Your will seeing Your presence in every step. Equally, may we travail steadfast in Your name by pureness, knowledge, long-suffering, and kindness by the Holy Ghost. Amen.

WALKING THE LIGHTHOUSE STAIRS

My brethren, count it all joy when ye fall into divers temptations;
Knowing this, that the trying of your faith worketh patience.

JAMES 1:2-3

Every time that I would try running up the lighthouse stairs with my brother or sister and/or neighbors, I would breathe harder than usual and stumble, barely missing the opportunities to fall down on several occasions as I often did. Soon, I deciphered that I should only attempt to walk the stairs instead. I have to admit, it would be different to arrive at the top a little bit later than everyone else. But the point of the matter was that I did get there eventually!

Exactly what was it that beckoned me to revisit the lighthouse atop the hill in Hannibal, Missouri, annually for several years? Generally, once a year preferably during the summer months on a Saturday, us kids would take a trek. Curiosity had caught our tails and upon seeing what was a humongous feat, we would endeavor to climb those steps leading up to the lookout point, windows in the lighthouse at the top of its stairs.

We wound around the stairs as we made our onward and upward climbs to the top to successfully look upon the free-flowing Mississippi River with its barges, Queen riverboat and other water vessels maneuvering themselves up and down the winding bends of the river. There were times when I felt secluded from the small group as they laughed and hollered with one another almost breathless from the climb. My mind deviated elsewhere as I was overcome by the serenity of the views from the lighthouse.

It was in those quiet and isolated moments when I began to hear the voice of God talking to me. We must have made the climbs from when I was about age 8 to 14. One needs to know that I was given the nickname Tubby from my parents probably around 5 or 6 if not younger, so therefore had been carrying extra weight on my body. Certainly, that did not help me with the climbs but I was absolutely mystified by everything looking so small and distant, yet beautiful with grand hills and winding valleys.

It was like God reassured me that despite my weight, He directed my steps in my daily life. He would help me to feel good about what I was doing such as helping to take care of my mother. When she would suffer a bout from her Sickle Cell Anemia Disease, I would stay up during the nights with her and rub her body down in Isopropyl Alcohol. Also, He reminded me that Momma told me that I had been blessed with healing hands from God as she would feel so much better afterwards.

And in church, I would sing in the choir and give God the glory in song for the uplifting of the congregation. I would go on to sing solos which gave peace to others. Again, He reminded me of this gift as well. In school during ninth grade, I competed in the Mahan Oratorical Contest because God gave me the courage and strength to assert my talent and skills and I ended up winning third place despite remedial reading classes in seventh grade. Therefore, the testing of my faith did result in patience which gave me freedom! Freedom to learn to like myself in spite of obstacles posed upon me by others.

It seemed that I had multiple trials placed in my life even then. There was so much societal and cultural emphasis placed on the negative stuff such as my being short and stubby, dark-skinned and I didn't have good hair like many other girls of my race. I was even compared to my sister by her boyfriends and some family members in my looks which didn't help my self-esteem quite frankly. It wasn't her fault as she was born the way she was and I was born the way in which I was. The ways in which God had formed us in His image.

I just felt that being in that lighthouse listening for God's loving voice did so much to comfort and reassure my being as a person of some significance. It was just so peaceful, revealing, and freeing for me. I saw things in life from different perspectives which I was able to digest and reflect on even though I couldn't share the hollowness of my soul with others as it just hurt so much and so deep. At least I had God to talk with in the lighthouse and as a result, joined church at age 12 due to the relationship which I had developed with Him atop the hill.

How often do we speak to God or listen for Him to speak to us and provide reassurance? Do we look to Him to help us decipher our trials and tribulations which we're going through, or do we linger along and alone in our own misunderstandings? Can we learn to lean and depend upon His words to give us wisdom, help, joy, and hope for a better understanding in life events? Do you believe that the testing of your faith produces patience and freedom to go the long haul?

Revelation: Know that God probably speaks to your heart more often than what one may want to acknowledge and obey.

Endeavor: May we seek to open our minds, bodies, and souls to Your voice so that we might grow greater in patience and become reassured in Your mercy and freedom for our lives.

Prayer: Dear Heavenly Father, please save us anyway in the depths of our sorrow and pity and give us deep-seated joy in You! Let us know that You embody Yourself in our being as we allow You, and that You seek peace and joy in our spirits as well as truth and justice in our souls. Amen.

ALMOST

Running to the deeper, unventured edge
without warning, "Carpe diem!" my nephew
jumped from the hot, concrete's surface
felt against the soles of his brown, warm feet.

Springing into a high-flying somersault,
head-on, he leaped into the pool's edge
undaunted by the body of water
that laid twelve feet before him.

As his aunt, I had been watching him
as I was skimming the water like usual,
but he grew tired with all of the familiarities
of being the youngest, least experienced and puniest.

So, his curiosity resolved to overtake
all that was previously considered
out of bounds and forbidden territory
as he silently ventured into the other side.

DONNA COLLIER RICKMAN

Others, his cousins had seen him jump,
tumbling, plummeting, and disappearing
into the water's gaping mouth as he
frantically gasped for life's breaths.

Thrashing at the water's tongue
repeatedly with both sets of limbs,
he had become unsure of his immediate bearings
as he desperately tried to regain boundaries.

All that he had known was quickly pushed aside
as bodily fluids began redirecting themselves
streaming quickly out from his nostrils
and other significant orifices.

Now crevassing through his clenched teeth,
I began to bear witness to his blue-tinged lips
while his body fought helplessly
against the urgency of the crisis at hand.

Diving into the water's hungry mouth,
I retrieved my nephew's limp body and
laid him gently onto the concrete's surface
against his cool and clammy skin.

Others too, had come out from the house
and helped with his resuscitation as just
moments before at age four, he had ventured
out into the pool's most shallow end and was safe.

Dipping his small feet, one by one into
the mysteriously cool and inviting water,
he suddenly unsnapped his flotation device
almost seizing his moment of buoyancy forever!

Written by Donna Collier Rickman

GRACE

(Unmerited Divine Approval
or Favor Given By God)

RUSTLING LEAVES

"By this my Father is glorified, that you bear much fruit; so you will be my disciples."

ST. JOHN 15:8 (NKJV)

Growing up in a small, rural town made everything seem so serene and simple. Experiencing the changing of seasons from the mild, gentle breezes of spring watching the newly formed buds sprout into their most colorful flowers to the hot, spiraling out of control summers.

Summers that would be filled to 100 plus degree temperatures while drinking icy-cold lemonade and tea, eating mustard potato, macaroni, Jell-O and lettuce salads at piping-hot barbecues, and watching people fishing and boating up and down the Mississippi River were just a few childhood remembrances.

And even though winter months had our days absorbed in preparing for Christmas, building snowmen, throwing snowballs, riding sleds and ice skating, and spring was filled with the most colorful flower beds of buds and blossoms with forever gushing rain showers, autumn was the season I loved most!

There was a warm fuzziness felt amongst the cooler temperatures of the season drinking both hot apple cider and chocolate with marshmallows while making Smores upon a burning wood fire at camp. And decorating the most orange and most varied-sized pumpkins while saying "Trick or Treat" to neighbors on Halloween wearing our outrageously, many times, homemade colorful costumes.

Finally, raking rustling leaves into piles to only jump in and separate the piles all over again. It was also a time of fall harvest of the many vegetables and fruits that would fill our tummies during church fellowships and family Thanksgivings.

Rustling leaves, a definite sign of God's grace to help make us ready for the new changes in our lives to come by showing kindness and mercy as God's disciples. Do we remember to thank God for His many blessings in our daily surroundings? If you could pick a favorite season during the year, what might it be and why? Can we rest assured in our lives as we grow in God's daily grace?

Revelation: May we forever welcome God's teachings within our hearts as His disciples.

Endeavor: May we all welcome the blessings of each season; especially autumn as we hear God's voice in the rustling leaves in the wind.

Prayer: Thanks, Lord, for getting us ready for each new day as we grow in grace. Help us come to see Your wondrous beauty found throughout the seasons and help us to embrace Your grace throughout the seasons in our Christian journey. Amen.

SIT STILL AND LISTEN

For this thing, I besought the Lord thrice, that it might depart from me. And He said unto me, My grace is sufficient for thee: for my strength is made perfect in weakness. Most gladly therefore will I rather glory in my infirmities, that the power of Christ may rest upon me.

II CORINTHIANS 12:8-9

Paul was constantly on the go spreading the gospel and sharing the good news of God as he travelled from this place to that with his apostles healing the people and making them whole again. Or giving food, water, and even more importantly, grace from God. Grace being defined as unmerited divine approval or favor given by God. Imagine, being on the receiving end of Paul and his apostles? Possibly, you thought a miracle had happened right before your very eyes as you knew that you felt, saw and experienced your trials differently, now receiving favor.

One might ask, "How could Paul impart Christ's grace to others being that he was just a man or so it seemed." But what we as readers and followers of Christ must remember is that we can all impart grace to others from Christ. We can witness the grace which God has imparted not only in others, but ourselves in doing His work here on earth in that in our own infirmities, we can grow and become strengthened through our weaknesses. Thank you, Lord!

One day as Paul decided to sit still and listen to the words of Christ, he realized that he had received by no means on his own, a thorn in his side. Certainly, in the Bible his thorn is not stated regarding what it was or how he obtained it. However, it is written in the scriptures that three times he had approached God asking Him to remove it, but He wouldn't. Instead, God told Paul that he had been given unmerited divine favor and that his strength would be made perfect by his own weakness. I am sure that this calmed Paul giving him a feeling of wholeness.

It seems then that Paul rationalized in his pain and solidarity, that he could survive, after all with the power of God resting upon him. How often have we just sat still and then listened for the words, the power, the majesty and grace of our Heavenly Father as He spoke words of peace to us to perform our tasks here on earth as we were found to be greatly favored in His eyes? Have we witnessed this experience to others or just remained silent?

The thought of acquiring or gaining more strength from our weaknesses almost seems the opposite of what we as humans might envision and believe could actually happen to us. It is an oxymoron to human behavior. But Paul goes on to say in II Corinthians 12:10 the following: Therefore, "I take pleasure in infirmities, in reproaches, in necessities, in persecutions, in distresses for Christ's sake; for when I am weak, then am I strong."

Our weaknesses should then be thought of as strengths for which we can draw upon in our daily lives. Not fall from grace instead. Who would have thought that we should interpret the scriptures in such a way as Paul describes which basically, enables us to live on, survive, and manifest God's favor in our daily living despite our ill health, failings, shortcomings, or improprieties?

Just how often do we search for the truth in the Bible, even if it seems to be indifferent to our thoughts upon its reading? Do we read and study the word of Christ daily to give us enough basis or factual information to continue reading and thus, resolve our uncertainties? How many have ever felt the unspeakable grace or unmerited favor in which I write about from the Lord?

Revelation: It is wonderful to know that we serve a great and loving Father who is sympathetic to our needs as we sit still and listen to His words.

Endeavor: May we find strength in our weaknesses as we find grace within ourselves according to God's will.

Prayer: Help us, Lord, to know what it is that you would have us to live, walk, and value in our lives so that we might manifest your teachings in the very lives of those for whom we touch in all manners physically, spiritually, and verbally according to Your essence in amazing grace. Amen.

TWO CUPS OF COFFEE

But the Comforter, which is the Holy Ghost, whom the Father will send in my name, he shall teach you all things, and bring all things to your remembrance, whatsoever I have said unto you.

ST. JOHN 14:26

I am most blessed to be married to my spiritual adviser, guide, and leader whom I knew some years before I married him. Most mornings, we drink our two cups of coffee... one for him and the other for me before we even begin our early morning prayer and devotionals. It seems to comfort us several times during the week as we listen to the God inspired words of several television evangelists who help boost our faith and encourage dialogue along the day.

However, the most holy enlightenment which we receive comes from the Comforter whom we know without a doubt has been sent by the Father. If you are a willing and able student, you can learn a lot from the Holy Ghost who does in fact teach us many things and bring into our remembrance, what the Father has revealed unto us. We just have to be willing servants to God's word and His will and learn to become graceful students.

According to Wikipedia, there are seven gifts of the Holy Spirit: wisdom, understanding, counsel, fortitude, knowledge, piety, and fear of the Lord which originated from Patrology or the study of early Christian writers who were designated as Church Fathers. What we do not understand, we ask God's guidance in such situations to then lead us to Hs Truth.

Certainly, to learn to discern or differentiate the seven gifts as presented above one from another, one would have to establish a covenant with the Father; if not in fact the Trinity as I am listening for God's voice to direct me in the writing of this text and provide me strength in discernment. Again, what we do not know, we need to be led to resources to help provide us with the needed answers and directions for our lives.

The Bible teaches us that in order to get wisdom, we need understanding in matters. Counsel is set forth before us through the Holy Spirit who comes to aide us as a Comforter in acquiring grace, wisdom, piety, and a reverence for the Lord. All we need to do is to be open to acquiring such knowledge through spiritual outreach and community associations and connections.

As written in Romans 8:9, "But ye are not in the flesh, but in the Spirit, if so be that the Spirit of God dwell in you. Now if any man have not the Spirit of Christ, he is none of His." Therefore, even though we dwell in a physical body, in order to be of the Holy Trinity, we have to allow the Holy Spirit to enter our being and live within us in our daily lives.

We might need to ask ourselves, "Is what we are receiving, learning, and doing, of the Holy Spirit?" Can we recognize His presence in others as well as ourselves? Has one taken the time to try and establish a relationship with our Heavenly Father above? What would it take to learn to be a willing servant of God? Can we find a church with a man or woman of God's cloth to aid us in our endeavor?

Revelation: Learn to recognize the Holy Spirit and embrace what He provides us.

Endeavor: May drinking our two cups of coffee inspire us daily to become even more abreast of the works of our Comforter sent by God.

Prayer: Teach us, Heavenly Father, to acknowledge the work of the Holy Spirit who dwells within us to find wisdom, understanding, counsel, fortitude, knowledge, piety, and fear of the Lord. Amen.

AMAZING GRACE

In all thy ways acknowledge Him, and He shall direct thy paths.
Be not wise in thine own eyes: fear the Lord, and depart from evil.

PROVERBS 3:6-7

"Amazing Grace shall always be my song of praise. For it was grace that brought my liberty. I'll never know just why He came to love me so. He looked beyond my faults and saw my needs. I shall forever lift my eyes to Calvary. To view the cross where Jesus died for me. How marvelous the grace that caught my falling soul. He looked beyond my fault and saw my needs." Lyrics above from the song He Looked Beyond My Fault, written by Dottie Rambo.

Grace is that unmerited favor which God has for us. And it is the abundant and amazing grace of God which seals our covenant to Him if firstly, we believe it and secondly, we follow Him! We who believe know that if we stay on a steady path of acknowledging our Heavenly Father as we go forth in our prayers and workday, then He shall direct our paths and we will depart from evil. We sincerely have to believe this wholeheartedly in our hearts.

It will not be a thing of possibly or probably, but without a doubt, we pledge our allegiance unto Him that in fact He shall direct our footsteps in all matters of our affairs. From our waking in the morning and the rising of the sun, until the going down of the sun unto our slumber throughout the night, we acknowledge that God is present, God is merciful, God is omniscient, and God is full of wisdom within our lives. We believe that He truly looks beyond our faults to see our needs.

We fear the Lord not believing that any harm will come upon us, but for the reverence we give to Him in all of our ways and all of our days of praising and glorifying Him. Jesus Christ is our great Messiah whom we praise without fail in directing our ways, words, and decisions for our lives. What God freely gives and provides us in spirituality, sanctity, and most amazing grace, we can only repay in obedience to Him.

Have we looked back at our lives and actually thanked God for intervening on our behalf in the midst of a problem or ordeal? Can we feel the amazing grace which He bestows upon us in our minds, hearts and souls to be readily able and available to be a faithful soldier in His army? Have you ever admitted that in acknowledging God, He does indeed direct your paths?

Revelation: We need to enliven ourselves with faith, wisdom, joy, and adoration to acknowledge the Lord.

Endeavor: Make amazing grace your song of praise daily as you look beyond your faults and see your needs.

Prayer: Help us to live in your will, Lord, as we depart from evil. Thank You for the grace which is unmerited favor in Your eyes which allows us to actually grow in humbleness with our relationship in You as You direct our footsteps in Christian discipleship. Amen.

HOPE

(To want something to happen or become true with much anticipation)

STALWART CONFIDENCE

And thou shalt be secure, because there is hope; yea, thou shalt dig a hole about thee, and thou shall take thy rest in safety. Also, thou shalt lie down, and none shall make thee afraid; yea, many shall make suit unto thee.

JOB 11:18-19

Araminta Ross later known as Harriet Tubman Davis, born around 1820 became a leading abolitionist and conductor on the Underground Railroad following the North Star. But the biggest quality which Harriet developed as an individual was a stalwart confidence born out of sheer courage and determination to set her people (slaves) free.

Leading slaves out of bondage as Harriet did was a life-threatening task and took pure hope in the Lord and His angels that they would be directed, guided and assured that when they laid down, they could feel perfectly safe cupped in the hands of our Father from above. Therefore, despite all that gathered around Harriet and her party afar or close, from slithering vipers to slithering demons posed as slave holders and owners ready to kill her at a moment's notice, she never gave up hope!

She became God's MOSES as a woman to forever wake up and lead her people out of bondage. Not God's bondage but man's bondage to hold on to something not his own... God's children. Harriet kept on course making over nineteen trips across that Mason-Dixon line and freeing over 300 slaves in their life journeys. All because she never gave up the fight believing and knowing that God was on her side and would deliver them safely time and time again to a new home in their Jerusalem.

How many times are we so close to the prize, but give up on hope that God will save us, deliver us and set us free from our many trials and tribulations out of fear? Why can't we follow God's star believing that we are being led in safety away from all hurt and harm to be redeemed? Who's stopping us from being saved? No one but ourselves. Think about it!

Revelation: Hope always in the Lord to gain stalwart confidence.

Endeavor: May we remember the vested hope of those who came before us for a better and new day in serving God.

Prayer: Dear Father, thank You for our confidence in You to overcome fear and faithfully have You by our sides knowing that with You, all things are possible and can be conquered according to the hope which we find in You. Amen.

UNTIL WE MEET AGAIN

Jesus said, Take ye away the stone, Martha, the sister
of him that was dead, saith unto him, Lord, by this time
he stinketh: for he had been dead four days. Jesus saith
unto her, Said I not unto thee, that if thou wouldest
believe, thou shouldest see the glory of God?

ST. JOHN 11:39-40

It was a time of good and evil that had been unfolding and experienced throughout every nook and corner of Jesus' life. The Pharisees had already gotten word of the many miracles which Jesus was performing and were ready to arrest if not exile or kill Him. Many sheep outside of Jesus' fold, simply did not believe and doubted that He was the Son of the living God able to perform miracles at the drop of a hat for the glory of His Father.

There seemed to remain much division amongst the Jews of Bethany, a town about fifteen furlongs off from Jerusalem concerning the death of Mary and Martha's brother, Lazarus. They believed like Martha and Mary that had Jesus been present at Lazarus' bedside when he was sick, He would have delivered Lazarus from certain death.

Jesus informed Martha upon meeting up with her before being led to his grave that Lazarus would raise up again and function again as a living being despite the fact that he had been deceased four days and his body and clothes would carry the stench of death. Jesus called for sister Mary as well who was at home with Jewish friends and family members who were in mourning over Lazarus' death to join them at his grave.

Martha and Mary both believed that Lazarus would indeed rise again because of the resurrection that was certain to happen on the last day. So, she and her sister Mary would just wait until meeting again all together in the afterlife caught up in glory.

But upon Jesus being led to Lazarus' grave at the cave, He wept. Jesus just wanted Martha to move away the stone so that He could enter. He cried out for the life of Lazarus to come forth bound in grave cloth on both his hands and feet. Jesus had Mary and Martha to unbound him as he walked out of the grave much to their amazement as witnesses to the glory of God on earth.

Many of the Jews present truly believed in Jesus' miracle thereafter. Others may have become dismayed, maybe even envious and angry of the power which lay therein of Jesus and skirted off telling the Pharisees what Jesus had done in resurrecting Lazarus from the dead. They probably just wanted to come into good favor with the Pharisees anyway as non-believers.

Do you believe in the power of Jesus to heal and bring back to life what was lost? Jesus died on the cross for our sins but before while walking the earth, interceded for our sins making atonement in His Father's name on our behalf. Are we true believers of the gospel according to Jesus? Or do we just believe and have faith when it conveniences us?

Revelation: Go forth as believers unto the gospel.

Endeavor: May we forever proclaim Your name, Father, and Your Son's name until we meet again!

Prayer: Allow us to become vessels of the living Christ here on earth, Father. Much of what was heard regarding the rising of their brother Lazarus back to life again from Jesus must have seemed as a dream for such a miracle to happen for Martha and Mary to witness. However, it was true as was the power of the Father which they witnessed that day. Amen.

BEATING DOWN SUN

Therefore, if any man be in Christ, he is a new creature: old things are passed away; behold, all things are become new. And all things are of God, who hath reconciled us to himself by Jesus Christ, and hath given to us the ministry of reconciliation.

II CORINTHIANS 5:17-18

And when I think of Christ, I do think in terms of redemption, renewal and reconciliation. That He, Jesus Christ died on the cross to save mankind from their sins and give them everlasting life in God our Father is redeeming and compromising in itself. I can't imagine what Jesus went through tied to that cross in the beating down sun to sundown. Exactly what kinds of things may have gone through His mind is only to be imagined although some of His words were heard and recorded.

Believers know that He asked forgiveness for the thief who died along beside Him on his own cross who believed in the Lord and Jesus forgave the people for what they had done in nailing His hands and feet to the cross crucifying Him for which He bore to His death, and was buried and rose again for our sins.

Also, that there were multitudes of people, believers and otherwise who witnessed such an atrocity against Jesus. Certainly, they only surmised that His death was imminent and forever never to be seen again. Who would have thought that Jesus would ever walk amongst men again even if in a different light and purpose through His disciples and apostles?

Therefore, how can we not be new creatures in Christ based on what He did to save our souls and bring us into everlasting life? Things that used to be are not absolute and no longer of importance in our living with and for Him. We actually should rebuild and reconnect our commitment to the covenant which we have with our Father in heaven because of Jesus. We need full reconciliation in God's word.

Our lives are not our own but those of God via His son, Jesus. To know that you are His child is to know the promises for which He has and continues to deliver to those of us who are His children so that we may come home to Him in glory.

Christians do not and should not exhibit an air of superiority such as being holier than others in Christ. Rather, draw nigh unto peace, humbleness, wholeness, and well-being in God, our Father. We must help Jesus to gather together His flock that they may be exalted in due time however the Lord directs their footpaths before their journeys' home.

Let Christians forever carry their crosses for the Lord as soldiers in His army while they carry the blood-stained banner honoring Jesus' death. Do we endure our crosses which Jesus bore for our sins? Is it time that we came to reconciliation with our status in the Lord?

Revelation: May we recognize our job in reconciliation with God through Jesus.

Endeavor: Let the beaten down sun remind us of the sacrifice which Jesus made for me and you.

Prayer: Help us to remember the price which Jesus paid for our transgressions and trespasses one against another. That we should always remember His sacrifices for us to His Father in redemption, renewal, and reconciliation for our sins which we carry daily on our own crosses. Amen.

QUITE FRANKLY

*Who has saved us, and called us with a Holy calling,
not according to His own purpose and grace, which was
given us in Christ Jesus before the world began.*

II TIMOTHY 1:9

Since I was a young child as I spoke about in my Introduction, I have felt a Holy calling from the Lord on my name, in my life, and works to be done while sojourning here on earth. I thank Jesus for the grace which He has given me to grow, develop, and mature into the person, wife, mother, grandmother, educator, writer, dramatist, lecturer, historian, and poet that I am becoming even now as I reflect and write.

Writing for me was not high on my agenda as a teenager. I liked English, reading, and writing but not to the point of writing a diary or thinking about a future memoir or personal essay. As a matter of fact, such thoughts and tasks had honestly not been even considered. After all, what did or could I have to write about that could become beneficial to the lives of others?

I most certainly loved speaking engagements and debates in junior high school having won third place in The Mahan Oratorical Contest. I also loved singing me some good Motown or Pop music of the seventies during Talent Shows at school. Luckily, I also was one of the main vocalists in a church band and the main vocalist in a pop/rock n' roll/ soul band in my youth. Therefore, I began to receive lots of public practice and attention in performance early.

However, to get through a great debate, one would need to do research and write out what seemed to be a short-lived dissertation on the subject matter at hand before memorizing the brief. I would work days on end trying to memorize, then vocalize through paraphrasing the words to then make for a most colorful and memorable presentation which was adjudicated by teachers and other outside judges before students and their families at school.

Luckily, the Lord has allowed me to write a children's story book which was published on January 29, 2021 as my first writing. Truly, I was inspired by so many people and thank God for such an opportunity. Now, this current book which I am writing, will be my next publication and one which I feel equally blessed as well in its production. I will say however, this has indeed been a challenge in itself from its conception to working into its completion.

Quite frankly, I have undergone some of the most ridiculous challenges in the simplest of logistics… everyday tasks to just begin, let alone keep the momentum going in the writing of this book. My other computer would simply shut down after a few plops on the keyboard. It was like it was so tired, it couldn't get enough energy to regenerate itself and stay working long enough for me to even get through a writing in one sitting. It was absolutely ridiculous, even with buying and using another charging cord. Finally, my son purchased me a new computer and files were transferred to it.

Throughout the course of writing these 99 commentaries, I suffered from various mishaps in my writings as I will attest to as follows. The Bible which I used to do my research, readings, and secure my scriptures, literally started falling apart from its covers to sections or by books. Therefore, I taped them back together. In my notetaking and document writing on notebook pages, I constantly encountered different challenges toward my work.

I suffered from coffee and bacon grease stains from slurped coffee or leakage from tops of pans since I worked at the kitchen table; engrained lipstick or jelly stains which somehow passed from my lips and fingers unto the notebook pages; I ended up making quite visible holes in my ink-penned note pages from hard pencil erasers and had to make repairs with tape again. What would I have done without it? Thank you, Jesus!

Truly, God has saved me again with a Holy calling and the anointed words which the Lord wants me to complete and allow others to hopefully read, reap, and learn from. I honestly believe that if God did not have a purpose for me in writing this book which I've felt throughout, then I would have simply quit eons ago for a self-published book. I pray that the words on these pages will provide insight, wisdom, testimony, and power to the greatness of God thus, make a difference in people's lives.

How many times have we been spiritually driven to perform a work but were feeling too overwhelmed or possibly incompetent to attempt, let alone complete it? Have we gone to God in prayer and listened to Him for His Holy calling as to how He wants us to proceed? Can we see beyond the glass ceiling and walk in His (God's) word? Can we believe that we are being called by a higher power than self in whatever task at hand needs to be performed?

Revelation: Thanks be to God as we listen for His Holy calling.

Endeavor: May we be open to the challenges in our life to make a difference toward mankind.

Prayer: May we know when God is anointing our words and work here on earth for the goodness and wellness of others. Likewise, may we remember that the good which we do here on earth shall be and is blessed according to our Father in Heaven. Amen.

FINDING MY PEN

*Yet if any man suffer as a Christian, let him not
be ashamed; but let him glorify God on his behalf.
Wherefore let them that suffer according to
the will of God commit the keeping of their souls
to Him in well doing, as unto a faithful Creator.*

I PETER 4:16;19

When I often think back and reflect on the times that man and Satan have wanted me to feel shame from acts not of God, but of men and women that have occurred against me as a Christian as well as others, I often think of the lyrics of the song below entitled, "He Touched Me."
"Shackled by a heavy burden, neath a load of guilt and shame.
Then, the hand of Jesus touched me and now I am no longer the same.
He touched me. Oh, He touched me and oh the joy that floods my soul.
Something happened and now, I know. He touched me and made me whole."

Sung by Gaither Vocal Band

Because of the above lyrics, it gives me reason to ponder and thank God for how He brought me through as a Christian, and why I prevailed coming out of the many situations, both physical and mental, which I overcame.

In doing such, I have frequently found my pen in writing about the specifics of the situation or placing other characters into a similar situation from which he, she or they escaped. Not all manuscripts have been published however. It's something I'm working on continuously as the Lord leads and guides me.

Also, I keep saying that I have found my pen in a specific genre but venture into another, then others as written and directed by God. I have written both in Fiction and in Non-Fiction in various genres: Juvenile Fiction, Devotionals, Middle-School Curriculum, Young Adults, Folk Tales, Adult Christian, Memoir, Personal Essay, Autobiography, Historical Fiction, Poetry, and Health Education. It seems that I make a stroke by His eyes and hands.

I do acknowledge and profess Jesus Christ as my Savior and know that without Him, I could not even think about being forgiven and redeemed from our Father, our Lord. It is like experiencing a big nightmare or dream sometimes that I awaken from and want to know if I am physically and mentally still existing on this plane called earth. My writings vary in story elements and storyline… often taking me to different surroundings, cultures, and adventures. Most often, I am hopeful that in trying to find my way out like being caught up in a maze, I most definitely escape Satan's snare.

Even in completing my writing of this book, I have had to extend my faith in ways which I never thought possible in revealing so many truths about myself and others and telling the stories of the characters found within the Bible. Some have been eye awakening and jaw dropping indeed.

Truly, God has challenged me in this venture and let me know more than once, that without leaning upon Him and giving Him the ultimate glory, my efforts would have been fruitless in finding my pen to write. He has literally directed my every stroke across the computer keys to allow me to write what I have heard from Him.

Revelation: I know that I have no shame in my blessed Savior as He is my all and all.

Endeavor: May we forever keep God in the forefront of all of our works and endeavors while giving Him the glory in our lives as we know that He is forever present directing our pens in our writing processes.

Prayer: Thank you, Lord, for the hope You give myself and other Christian writers in our daily walk with You while finding our pens. Without Your guidance and soulful inspiration, where would we be in our writing journeys? Thanks for helping us to find Your light our dear Creator. Amen.

DONNA COLLIER RICKMAN

TURNING POINT

For I know the thoughts I think toward you, says the Lord,
thoughts of peace and not of evil, to give you a future and a hope.

JEREMIAH 29:11 (NKJV)

Early one morning while washing the dishes, I heard the Lord speak just as clearly as anything saying, "Go forth, woman, you are not disabled anymore!" At first, I thought myself uncertain about the choice of words spoken unto me, but I heard them repeated again, "You are no longer disabled. Go forth and tell the good news!" So, immediately, I ran into various rooms of my house, then outside just giving praises to the Lord and crying tears for His revelation.

Immediately, my mind flashed back to moments of hospitalization for my Post Traumatic Stress Disorder which resulted in major depression, crippling anxiety and amnesia. However, my thoughts now are that I can function as being less disabled based on society's norms. At least not according to my doctor's diagnoses and treatments, but to the diagnoses and wellness of the Lord! For He is the head and director of my life story here on earth. Not man or woman, but God, Himself!

This is my turning point to let go and let God. Discernment through the workings of the Holy Spirit helped me to remember the words of the Lord, to give me thoughts of peace and not of evil and of hope and a future. To work well within the realm and beyond of my disorder as so many people with my disabilities do every day. Certainly, nothing that has happened to me, has not happened before to others. No, I am not alone in this challenge.

Knowing that I can function positively and remain constructive through writing books and giving lectures and seminars; talking with both children and adults; working in my church, serving on boards within and outside my community, and sharing my experiences about how I overcame with the Lord's help and direction through daily prayers of humbleness and thanksgiving. Therefore, I will immediately go forth in victory! With God our Father on my side, I can only win.

I will talk with my doctor and let him know the joy of healing which I have felt and witnessed on this blessed morning to have my medications and therapy reduced as I know that I still need them to function, but not to survive. I will tell him that I am ready to be healed and whole, able to live, work and have a more productive and functioning life and do just that. I will prevail with the Lord's help... this I know for the Bible tells me so! I will not be a statistic of life's changes and challenges.

How many times have we discounted the words of the Lord, thus missing our blessings? Shall we look back and reflect upon these things listening to His words to take us into fulfilment in our lives? Or shall we live trapped in what we think a disability looks, feels, and sounds like? What are you waiting for? Fly into the glory of God's goodness for our lives!

Revelation: We do have a hope and a future in Jesus Christ!

Endeavor: Keep thoughts of peace and one's ability to function close by.

Prayer: Learn to listen to the Lord and follow His lead. Know that He is with us and directing us according to His word and would never harm us. Only prosper us whether it be in wealth, health, and other attributes becoming of Himself for the betterment of our lives. Amen.

JOY

(A State of Happiness or
Cause of Delight)

RESOUNDING JOY

"My brethren, count it all joy when you fall into various trials, knowing that the testing of your faith produces patience."

JAMES 1: 2-3 (NKJV)

Over forty-five years ago my sister gave birth to a healthy baby boy named Frankie, but it turned out that his umbilical cord was wrapped around his neck which resulted in severe oxygen loss to his brain and the crippling effects of cerebral palsy and dystonia throughout his entire body. What was once joyous seemed ruthlessly tragic for moments there following his birth as her faith in fact produced patience.

As my nephew Frankie grew, his head as well as upper torso and legs had to be fastened into his wheelchair so he wouldn't fall out. However, he would forever be smiling the whole time through without a care or worry seemingly felt throughout his crippling body. Truly, he was a child of God's and quite a blessing to all whom he touched in his life until his passing at age five.

My sister was a commissioned officer in the United States Air Force and was already quite challenged by her military duties. She was also married and had two step-children at home to care for and raise. There were so many times that she showed courage and fortitude amid days of tireless trials as her faith was sorely tested, yet her patience prevailed.

There was much heartache and many sleepless nights but thank God for His resounding joy felt in the depths of my sister's heart in the morning. She was a trooper and embraced life as it came! Truly, she has been a role model for her siblings, church family, military families, and community. As a mother, she rocked the earth as her faith and joy shined forth in her son.

Might we all find the true meaning of joy to carry through in all of our challenges set before us in our daily walk in Jesus' name? Can we recall a time when we felt resounding joy in spite or despite a situation or thing that seemed to stand so firmly in our way? Can we see and feel joy in the depths of our heart regardless of our circumstances? Might we learn to remind ourselves of the strength of hope and resilience which we grow according to our faith in the Lord and Jesus.

Revelation: Faith is joyful hope; sharing such joy with others around and in your lives.

Endeavor: May we look for resounding joy that can be seen and heard all around us in our homes, neighborhoods, and communities.

Prayer: When it seems that we have done all that we can, cleave even closer to our faith in joy. Help us, Lord, to know that patience will prevail throughout the duration of our trials helping us to make it through in Your precious name. Amen.

RISING SUN

From the rising of the sun to its going down,
the Lord's name is to be praised.

PSALM 113:3 (NKJV)

Each morning from the sun's rising in my daily encounters with God, I give honor, thanks, and praise to my Heavenly Father. I sit upright on my knees or stand accordingly as I hear Him calling my name to rise and shine…basking in His most abundant glory! I cannot thank Him enough for another day's journey in the life of Christ. Praises be to the Lord!

I listen as He utters to me my tasks for the day; especially in the morning. They might be to take a thirty-minute brisk walk, drink a cup of hot tea, have a quick check-in with my daughter on the telephone, say my prayers for my children and grandchildren for the day on their travels to and from their schools or daycare and workplaces, make sure that my husband is ready to awaken and get ready for his day as I then serve us breakfast.

Here and there, I chuckle from time to time as God's words ring humorously throughout my ears and I just have to laugh out loud. At other times. His name almost pierces my eardrums and I just have to repeat again and again, "Thank you, Jesus. Thank you Lord! Hallowed be Your name," and speak the Lord's Prayer in praise as I prostrate myself before Him on the floor or cushions.

And throughout the rest of the day, something may spontaneously cause me to praise Him such as an unexpected phone call from a dear friend or relative whom I've not heard from in weeks; sometimes, months. Most definite, praises in entering another or several devotional page(s) to my book. Or possibly, an unexpected visit from someone to my home or destination outside of the home.

Of course, we have to thank and praise Him for our other meals for lunch and dinner as there are those who don't always have food to eat on a regular basis during mealtimes and we need to always be cognizant of that with the Covid 19 virus and loss of jobs, incomes, and homes for families, not only nationwide but worldwide.

After dinner, I sometimes get back on the computer and write more commentary for my book or watch the latest in news topics or a television program. Wherever and whatever I am directed to go and do in the evening, I usually do that in honor to our Father.

Towards night's end after the events of the day, I set up my pallet with cushions and sprawl myself out before God in a prone position either on my back or stomach and thank Him for how good He was to me on this day. And every day!

Can't everyone reading this passage give God some praise for how good He's been to you and your family and friends in light of what is going on in the world around us? Shall we forever remain thankful to our Father in heaven for His mighty works in our lives? Isn't it just wonderful to start and end our day with our Heavenly Father in prayer?

Revelation: God didn't have to wake us up and bring us through to another beautiful day!

Endeavor: Watch God change things, yet add consistencies to our lives if we just embrace the clarity of mind, beauty of life, and serenity of our spirits in Jesus' name from sunrise to sunset.

Prayer: Joyous praises to the Lord who makes a way for all things we encounter. May we habitually awaken to the newness and glory of life, liberty, and the pursuit of happiness in our coming and going through the will of our Lord daily. Amen.

LAUGHING AGAIN

When the Lord turned again the captivity of Zion, we were
like them that dream. Then was our mouth filled with
laughter, and our tongue with singing: then said them among
the heathen, The Lord hath done great things for them.

PSALM 126:1-2

Think of the times when you felt captive by a thing or things. Whether
drugs or alcohol, sins of the flesh, greed for or love of money, homes,
cars, jewelry, idols and so forth. What let you know the difference
between being held captive by it or just enjoying it for your pleasure and
indulgence since you earned that right by hard work, study, and strife?
Not seen as sinful in nature.

Much of the above is what had happened to the people of Zion
when God allowed their captivity by King Nebuchadnezzar. They had
decided to put life as they knew it into their own hands and shunned
the teachings of God which they were taught to believe and follow. Now
they were as lost sheep on the prairie without their shepherd leading
them.

I'm sure that following the twist in the plot which thickened
after the Lord placed His hands back into the mix with all captivity
surrounding about them, they probably did feel like they were in a deep
dream unimaginable to man. Suddenly, reality hit and they became
immersed in pure joy and laughter as funny and excitable or possibly,
rigid and bizarre in nature as it all seemed.

Think on this. All of the control, hardening of hearts, disrespect, and gross negligence on the part of the king and his militia toward Zion dissolved in minutes after the Lord had deemed worthy their presence from all of the sins committed against Him believing they now earned their right to freedom again.

Remember that the heathen people laughed thanking God, singing praises, and becoming restored in His truth. The reality hit them that had it not been for the Lord and His forgiving grace, love, patience, and care for their overall welfare, then where would they have been but kept in captivity still.

So, they came to know through their personal experiences, the greatness of the Lord in what He had done for them and grew greatly appreciative. I wonder if it was like a chain reaction which went through the crowd or were they simply listening for the voice of God as they hollered out for forgiveness and redemption?

Had your people been caught up in captivity, how easily could you have faced reality and then laughed? When do you think the people of Zion finally rejoiced after discovery of such truths? Could you and others in your own family see yourselves in this story, yet filled with joy and triumph afterwards?

Reflection: Think about ways which we have placed ourselves into captivity away from God.

Endeavor: To fervently work toward freedom so that we may share in the reality of laughter and joy forevermore in the Lord.

Prayer: Pray to the Lord for freedom from our self-made captivities knowing that we have free-will to just let go and surrender ourselves, letting God take control of our destinies believing that He has all power in His hands. Amen.

ROLL THEM UP

Praise ye the Lord, O give thanks unto the Lord; for
He is good: for His mercy endureth forever.

PSALM 106:1

Walking the paper route every Saturday morning delivering rolled up newspapers was like the early morning cops who we would see working their early morning beats generally by car. We both saw each other and it was a slight head nudge that one cop in particular would give to say "Good morning!" Every Saturday morning our ritual was to roll them up and place rubber bands on them between 5:00-5:30 under the direction of my cousin Blackwell who was a woman almost in her seventies. Now, this was not a task to be taken lightly as my cousin who seemed more like a great aunt and army sergeant was very regimented and deliberate in such an obligation which I deemed as necessary to our nation. Granted she got paid some dollars and cents for her efforts.

Let it be known that we would be in prayer as well each morning after rolling them up before our scheduled deliveries. Most times, Cousin Blackwell would recant verses which she knew word for word and had more than memorized but imbedded into her heart and soul right from the Bible's pages. Praise ye the Lord, O give thanks unto the Lord; for He is good: for His mercy endureth forever. She was a strong woman and armed in the faith of God knowing that through Him, all things were possible and despite the racial unrest which was happening within the nation as well as our own hometown… would be overcome in God's time, not our own time.

Area residents opening and reading the newspaper in the early morning was just as common as eating home-baked apple pie for Sunday dinner as it seemed most homes had delivery services within our designated areas. And who was not ready to be enlightened to the national news and headlines as well as local news happening in our area communities. No matter if criminally-involved cases, obituaries, or situations affecting us directly within those reporting moments. Everyone read the newspapers it seemed and wanted to be informed by the best source available to man as Hannibal was one of your rural, mail free delivery communities in Marion County. The rubber bands we used to roll the newspapers up were sturdy, yet highly flexible, ready to eat those newspapers up in having them performing all kinds of gymnastics adhering to rolling.

Us kids and Cousin Blackwell worked diligently in our tasks at hand and felt major responsibility to be the best paper girl, woman, and boy carrier on any route. Thank God for the hearing of His word for everyone to jump to a spring and get grounded in the delivery of our services daily. Plus, we would oftentimes get a little something in an envelope at Christmastime from the mailboxes for our services which was greatly appreciated, especially by our cousin. Of course, the biggest treat was us getting twister doughnuts after the route every Saturday at the local bakery without fail. They were so big and sugary to eat. Delicious, yum, yum!

Did you ever feel such faith and joy in a task such as simply rolling newspapers up? Do you sense God's presence in all that you do no matter how great or small? Have you ever felt that your tasks had gone unnoticed and not worthy of being noticed by your employer or fellow employees? Has there ever been a relative of yours as joy-filled with the Holy Spirit as I described Cousin Blackwell to have been? Did you ever let him or her know how much he or she enriched your own life?

Revelation: Make us aware that every task we do in our lives holds significance for someone else.

Endeavor: May we always remember those family members who came before us and led the way in great role-modeling for our lives.

Prayer: Thank you, Lord, for allowing everyone to be an agent of change for happenings in this world. Remind us that we are Your gatekeepers and with Your guidance even in the smallest of tasks...can soar and make a difference in others' lives. Amen.

LOVE PASSING ACROSS CULTURES

Love can be so vibrant and colorful,

passing across all cultures.

Then, becomes shrouded over by all shades of gray.

Charcoal gray,

Light gray,

Gray haze,

Blue gray,

All becoming

GRAY

Absurdities,

Blunders,

Inconsistencies,

Incompetences,

Prejudices,

and

Maladies

As gray matter brews throughout a forlorn sky

and once beautiful backdrop.

Written by Donna Collier Rickman

LOVE

(Strong Affection for Another
from Kinship, Personal Ties,
Admiration or Common Interests)

LOVE HEALS ALL

Beareth all things, believeth all things,
hopeth all things, endureth all things.

I CORINTHIANS 13:7

Sojourner Truth was known as Young Isabella. A girl who although born into slavery around 1797, was also sold four times into slavery as a child. The first time she was just nine years old and was sold to a master on the auction block who spoke a different language- English from her low Dutch. She was taken out to his barn and beaten with hot rod irons on her back because she did not speak the same language so she could not understand his commands. This scarred her for life, but she was determined to move forward remembering the words of her parents Mau Mau Bett and PaPa Baumfree to tarry on and look to God to help her.

Despite Isabella's separation from her family, she married and had five children although having been abused physically, mentally, and emotionally by several slave masters. She then walked to freedom with her baby daughter in her arms. Then, hearing a calling from God Himself, she changed her name to Sojourner Truth as she was to sojourn the roads, campsites and towns and for a short time before moving to the next location. She would tell the people of their sins and about the truth of the Lord.

During her lifetime, Sojourner won three court battles and received monetary compensation for each case. She was the first African American woman to challenge her case of her five-year old son being illegally sold down South in a white courtroom and won her case against a white man. She also helped desegregate the streetcars in Washington, D.C. after having two conductors fired for actions against her. Likewise, she won a slander case against a minister in New York who accused her of poisoning another minister to his death.

In all of that, she became a great abolitionist and speaker for women's rights, anti-slavery, temperance, capital punishment and societal issues in America. She befriended great suffragists, Elizabeth Cady Stanton and Susan B. Anthony and abolitionists, Frederick Douglass and William Lloyd Garrison. She also met with two great American Presidents, Abraham Lincoln and Ulysses S. Grant in trying to better serve the needs of the freedmen (black soldiers) and their families in Washington, D.C. from their fight in the Civil War to obtain needed medical care, land, homes, and education.

Now Sojourner was a loving person who bore, believed, hoped and endured all sorts of trials for the sake of the Lord and others in her healing as well as the well-being of her people. She helped to save souls and bring them to Christ as well. Likewise, she challenged herself with so many societal issues affecting so many people. So why can't we as Christians do the same? How many times have we wanted to speak out on behalf of the Lord or some issue of utmost importance in our lives and family? Sojourning for the truth of the Lord isn't always easy, but like Sojourner can't we share the gospel with all those whom we meet and help them on and in their pathway to heaven?

Revelation: Be a sojourner of God's truth and love bearing, believing, hoping, and enduring all things.

Endeavor: Help us, Lord, like Sojourner Truth in her tireless efforts and endurance to fight for your truth and justice in all things.

Prayer: Thank You, God, for allowing us to be witnesses to Your greatness to the point whereby, we share such love, comfort, and hope with our fellow man and woman, girl and boy in Christ! In turn, as they learn God's love and truth…they may further share the greatness of Christ with others as well while sojourning in Your truth. Amen.

BETWEEN FRIENDS

And whatsoever ye shall ask in my name, that will I do, that the Father may be glorified in the Son.

ST. JOHN 14:13

Between friends, there is so much unwritten and unvoiced communication which takes place within their relationships. Communication which sometimes can seem made up or coded in such a fashion that others cannot penetrate that bond. I must substantiate my title to include *best* friends because this is where the spiritual binding takes place between words, actions, and allegiances.

Basically, we say to each other in our relationships what this verse says from Jesus to God. And whatsoever ye ask in my name I will do for you, Father. That is essentially what *best* friends do and say both written and unwritten between one another. They shelter, yet trust, honor and cherish one another for the gift which he or she has been given and received.

We thank God for enabling us to form a union many times that no man can put asunder like in a marital vow or pledge to one another to the point of dying for a *best* friend. Unquestionably, God does not ask us to die for Him although there are those among us who would simply, without question… do just that so that our Holy Father may be glorified in the Son.

Yet, still the love and devotion which exists between *best* friends can sometimes be just as powerful as the love which exists between siblings to be exact! I can attest to such friendship as I have witnessed it myself unfold and develop to such a degree as it has. Truly, it has been ordained according to the Father in heaven and blessed as such through His Son, Jesus Christ.

When one has been so fortunately blessed, he or she can't help but fall on one's knees and praise the Lord daily for such a relationship as this by saying, "Thank you Jesus. Thank you Lord!" What remains in such a union are the bountiful effects of wonder, realism, laughter, sadness, and truism to one's self and his or her *best* friend.

Ask yourself, "When was the last time or first time for that matter when you thanked the Lord through His Son, Jesus for your beautiful friendship between you and your *best* friend? How often do you praise him or her for what love, joy, insight, and depth is bestowed directly to you from them to you? What can we do to maintain the integrity of our relationship no matter how old or new to then share such knowledge, discernment, and trust which we have acquired through our special friendship with others?

Revelation: Thanks be to God for how He has blessed our lives for the love, trust and sanctity of a *best* friend.

Endeavor: Make it a goal for us to help form relationships such as ours between friends.

Prayer: May we be mindful of the gift of friendship given to us every day that we may ask Jesus to give us the needed thoughts, words, and skills to then ask of His Father in Heaven to enable us to proceed and work in His name so that Jesus might glorify Him. Amen.

LOVING YOU IS BEAUTIFUL

He that hath my commandments, and keepeth them, he it is that loveth me: and he that loveth me shall be loved of my Father, and I will love him, and will manifest myself to him.

READ ST. JOHN 14:15

This verse acknowledges that Jesus and God are one together. In other words, Jesus said that when we see Him as when He appeared on the earth with His disciples and prophesized and healed the people, then we saw the Father as well. Likewise, we cannot acknowledge God without referring to His Son, Jesus Christ. To say that one really loves the Lord is to admit that there is no one above Him that we celebrate, honor, and exalt greater in all of heaven and earth.

He is the One who created man and woman and breathed life into our nostrils. God is the Alpha and the Omega, the beginning and the ending, the Genesis and the Revelation as spoken and inspired in the pages of the King James version of the Bible. But, most importantly, He sacrificed His only begotten Son's life for our salvation as Jesus hung on the cross for our sins and transgressions.

We must remember that after Jesus' death, He laid in His grave for three days before arising and being seen walking, talking, and teaching His disciples some truths about how they should be instructed to carry on His work and ministries until His return. Jesus left ascending up into Heaven and since has sat at the right hand of God, His Father.

Jesus says then to them who keep His commandments that if they follow and obey them, then they love Jesus and His Father. Therefore, will they both love the people who have become disciples of God's truth and loves them both. And thereafter, will Jesus forever love them and make His essence known to man. We just have to be willing to embrace Him.

You may wonder or ask yourself, "How does Jesus manifest Himself to us as mere man and woman; girl and boy?" And I would say through His many works and miracles as witnessed daily right before our eyes. Equally, in our prayers the great love which He has for us shines through our daily encounters with animals, children, men and women. Many times, if we but listen, we can hear his response to our concerns. And most certainly, if we just watch and wait upon Him… we receive our answers in due time.

Exploring new destinations in space and below the sea; conquering new heights and depths upon the earth; teaching our children the meaning of life, waking up each morning and taking another breath, surviving the coronavirus and other illnesses and challenges physically, mentally, monetarily, and otherwise to then witness and tell about how you made it through with the Lord's help. Thank you, Jesus! How can loving You be anything but beautiful.

Do you believe that Jesus appears to you today in other forms? Do you think that you could or would recognize Him and what He stands for in other human beings, animals, and etc.? What are you waiting for when it comes to giving God and His son the honor, glory, and praise for all that they do for us in our daily lives? Could others tell how much we love them and what our relationship with Him and the Father means to us based on our relationship to them?

Revelation: Acknowledge God, the Father and His Son, Jesus Christ equally as they are one.

Endeavor: Loving you, Lord, and your Son, Jesus is beautiful because it simply is! No questions asked.

Prayer: May we forever remember that You both loved us before we loved ourselves. It is through Your example, words inspired in the Bible and commandments that we are directed to receive our gifts in the Spirit. Help us to recognize and acknowledge Your presence all around us and in us for the betterment of Your children. Amen.

EATING TOGETHER

And ye shall teach them your children, speaking of them
when thou sittest in thine house, and when thou walkest by
the way, when thou liest down, and when thou risest up.

DEUTERONOMY 11: 19

Eating together at the supper table used to be considered in earlier centuries, a must have and do especially depending upon the culture you were from. It was a normal tradition to have family members sit down at the table during dinnertime especially, and eat together. And of course, depending upon what the current state of affairs and activities everyone was involved with, would result in staples of discussion and possible decision-making. Indeed, everyone had a stake at the table regarding his or her welfare. No one was without responsibility to handle aspects of the family unit in and out of home structure.

Most recently during the last ten to fifteen years, with what has become known as ridiculous family schedules because of the children's activities such as sports, dance, music, arts, gym, athletics, drama, and so forth, family times of sitting down and eating together have become sparse. Sometimes, even a thing of the past because of current states of health and wellness resulting in cases and deaths from the coronavirus or Covid 19. Such a virus has resulted in millions of cases however, allowing families to reemerge and come back together at the dinner table.

Through the years, it seemed that such an entrusted family ritual was just that… considered as a sanctified duty for maintaining integrity, viability, and validity of such an institution called the family. It was a time to talk about the activities of the day and how one got through them with or without incident. Family members could talk about winning and disappointing moments which transpired throughout their day. Or possibly, a parent could get family consensus concerning an important choice or decision which would in most cases, affect the entire family and its current scheduling of at home or away activities needed to take place.

Even in taking into account The Last Supper which Jesus held with His disciples was a time of transition, unity, and business. He basically had a mental checklist when they all sat down at the table and began giving instructions and tasks which each disciple should be responsible for in completing. I am sure that there was possibly some discord noted amongst the group concerning such tasks designated by Jesus. Who knows, there could have been some disagreements regarding such or means by which such tasks were to be completed and by whom.

You know, like the normal polarity which occurs in today's families. No different, folks. I am sure that Jesus had a way to bring consensus and cohesiveness immediately home to the disciples. Everyone knew his value and significance in mankind at the table with plenty of work or tasks that had to be completed. Something tells me that all felt important in his role because of Jesus being at the head like a parent directing things. Parents whether father or mother-led are at the head of the household in charge of all chores, activities, and roles as we know in most societies.

Although they were grown men, how could Jesus not have felt that He didn't have more buy-in, reflection, and responsibility at the helm of the ship in His disciples' awakenings, walking by, and lying down at the end of each day? There had to be a reckoning and account of each disciple's checklist of completion. Correct in order to have a running account from everyone so to speak in the family.

How often do you praise the times in which you and your family members can sit down at the dinner table or eat meals and interact together? What about the dent which Covid 19 has made in our family time today; have you used this time as an advantage point in family unity? What significance do you think Jesus played in The Last Supper to His disciples? Do you think that eating together strengthens the family unit in teaching about Jesus and family values?

Revelation: Look at one's meal times and determine their importance in one's life.

Endeavor: May all family members come to know the value they play in the functioning and well-being of their families.

Prayer: Parents and designated adults, ask God for discernment, understanding, and wisdom while instructing one's family unit. May each family member feel exalted as an important element in his or household to then share one's thoughts, concerns, victories, challenges and changes in the functioning of their daily lives. Amen.

LOYALTY

(Faithful to a Cause, Ideal,
Custom, Institution or Product)

WITHERING HEIGHTS

For God so loved the world, that he gave his only begotten Son, that whosoever believeth in him should not perish, but have everlasting life.

ST. JOHN 3:16

Nationally in the United States and the world there is a definite decline, fundamental downward shift or withering heights associated with those individuals who practice Christianity as observed and spoken by religious leaders and witnessed throughout church edifices today. Such buildings are becoming scarce or greatly lessened by believers to a larger extent than ever before.

Although there are becoming far more religious denominations and doctrines; "agnostics who claim neither faith nor disbelief in God, and atheists who attest to disbelief in the existence of God, a higher power or spiritual force of any kind" according to Merriam-Webster Dictionary, many people still claim their faith and loyalty in the trinity of the Father, Son, and Holy Spirit.

For God gave His only begotten Son, a singular child named Jesus who died on the cross which He bore for you and me. God knew before our great Messiah's birth of His impending doom some 33 years later; arising from the dead to sit at the right hand of his Father and glorify Him in heaven and thus, save mankind from their sins.

Anything that we ask in His Son, Jesus' name we can receive from the Father. With those words in mind, how can anyone for that matter, not believe in God. And with the help of the Holy Bible, God's inspirationally-sanctified reflections and writings, we have a daily guide to instruct, lead, and direct our footsteps as to how and or when we should proceed along our life's journey while here on earth.

Possibly, those who are non-Christians need a word from the Lord to seize the opportunity to serve Him? They may be as doubting Thomas who needed proof of the power and existence of God and how He could invoke His promises to be known to man. It may be a leap of faith to radically take such an oath to change one's belief making a covenant with a higher power of holiness and majesty.

The Heavenly Father is a Savior we can believe in, depend upon, and follow fulfilling and sustaining us. Does being a Christian test one's faith in God? Will Christianity make a comeback anytime soon in popularity amongst the masses? Will sharing our story as Christians to non-believers make a difference… drawing them closer to God's word? How does the Bible differ from other religious beliefs and doctrines in order to enable it to reign as the ultimate word in the United States, let alone the world?

Revelation: Despite withering heights in popularity, knowing one's eternity as a Christian is a blessing for sure!

Endeavor: May we prove to be ambassadors in Christ for the world to witness.

Prayer: Thank you, Father, for your Son, Jesus who died on the cross to save us from our sins and give us everlasting life. What better gift can we imagine differently that will be so enlightening and fulfilling in our spiritual departure from this earthly plane? Amen.

JUST A CLOSER WALK

And He said, Thou canst not see my face: for there shall no man see me, and live. And the Lord said, Behold, there is a place by me, and thou shalt stand upon a rock: And it shall come to pass, while my glory passeth by, that I will put thee in a cleft of the rock, and will cover thee with my hand while I pass by: And I will take away mine hand, and thou shalt see my back parts: but my face shall not be seen.

EXODUS 33: 20-23

What a relationship that Moses shared with the Lord! From his conception onto his birth and further into the twist of turn which Moses took in being hidden three months after his birth by his mother, Jochebed and adopted by Pharaoh's daughter. Quite ironically, his mother became his wet nurse and the rest was history as Moses was not killed by the Pharaoh at his birth as many readers may ponder.

God had a greater purpose for Moses way before Moses came to realize and accept it and lead the way for his Hebrew or Israelite people to a different awakening and presence before the Lord. These people who had fallen into hard times and divisive ways contrary to the ways of the Lord were now being given a new choice and chance as to how to live and serve their Holy Father.

The Lord, God brought Moses' unruly clan out of Egypt and into Mount Horeb where they eventually built their camps within the Tabernacle which would be truly unacceptable to Christ. Moses immediately separated the two sites and set the Tabernacle of the congregation afar off from the campsites and as he entered it, and the people marveled from afar as to what would happen with him.

God was about to appear to Moses in the sanctity of the Tabernacle as a cloudy pillar as He did not want him to look upon His face in glory and die. Therefore, God led him outside to safety and had him stand upon a rock where He later put him in its cliff while God covered him with His hand as he passed by him viewing only His back parts and never God's face.

Just a closer walk with God manifested itself right before Moses' eyes! He could not have gotten any closer than that. How Moses could be so privy to be chosen by the Lord, God Himself to witness such a miracle was beyond his wildest imaginations. God entrusted in him so much to bestow such honor and majesty upon His son, Moses, to ultimately lead His people out of bondage.

I cannot imagine such the moments, but every living thing must have breathed the freshness of the crisp air as they saw a most magnificent light only known to encompass the glory of the Lord, God Himself full and divine and beyond any known recognition to man. What glory, what omnipotence, and what manifestation to behold with God's presence right in the midst of everyone and everything which He had created known to man in those precious moments.

Glory Halleluiah as the people laid down palms while shouting, "Hosanna in the highest! Blessed be the Lord." Giving all honor, praise, magnification, and glory to Him as He passed by. Remember, Moses could not have gotten any closer and lived while his people marveled and wondered what was taking place right before their eyes!

Just a Closer Walk With Thee lyrics go as follows:

"I am weak but thou art strong. Jesus keep me from all wrong.
I'll be satisfied as long, As I walk, let me walk close to Thee.
Just a closer walk with Thee. Grant it Jesus, is my plea.
Daily walking close to thee. Let it be, dear Lord, let it be."
Sung by Patsy Cline and Willie Nelson

How many of us can say that in loyalty, we walk daily with Jesus? Certainly, not the way in which Moses did but by faith? Do we thank

God for the air that we breathe and the breaths that we take upon our awakening and sleeping? Are we thankful for our daily blessings of family and friends, life, health, food, shelter, and thanksgiving? Do we many times just assume that these are givens and by whom as nothing is promised but our blessed meeting with God if we believe in Him and accept His Son Jesus, who died on the cross for our sins?

Endeavor: May we remember to give God His glory in all facets of our daily living.

Revelation: As we walk, let us remember to be vigilant to walk in step, in faith, and most importantly, in loyalty to you.

Prayer: Dear Heavenly Father, please help us to remain faithful and honest in Your sight we pray. Help us to remember Moses and the Israelites in how they overcame and found victory in You, oh Lord. May we await to see Your most precious, sacred, and glorious face when we meet You in the rapture. Amen.

SOME PEOPLE

To speak evil of no man, to be no brawlers, but gentle, shewing
all meekness unto all men. For we ourselves also were sometimes
foolish, disobedient, deceived, serving divers (various) lusts and
pleasures, living in malice and envy, hateful, and hating one
another. But after that the kindness and love of God our Savior
toward man appeared. Not by the works of righteousness which
we have done, but according to His mercy He saved us, by the
washing of regeneration, and renewing of the Holy Ghost.

TITUS 3:2-6

It seems only natural to be found within our human nature to make
judgement against any and everything not common to one's self,
livelihood, personality, socio-economic status, chosen line of work,
and other presenting opportunities. Therefore, men and women,
teenagers, girls and boys can be heard daily speaking evil toward
their fellow brother, sister, neighbor, friend, and foe. That is the evil
which lies embedded within many, if not most of our hearts. Evil
which needs and pleads the help of the Holy Spirit to be spit out and
us made whole.

Only, on rare cases does our nature turn the other cheek toward such
rubbish and not assume or make our own filtrated judgements towards
another's character, situation or condition. Yes, that would result in
some people who can outwardly and genuinely find or show meekness,
kindness and the love of our Savior towards all others forfeiting their
own judgements toward others. I can't even imagine Heaven here on

earth with everybody loving each other and building one another up in the sight of God!

Truly, the earth is just that, a planet in service to mankind for all of men's and women's needs to be fulfilled no matter the cost. Costs in human suffering brought forth by others, our living conditions including type of car driven down to the house or apartment in which one lives is looked upon with great envy and hatefulness toward others. Even to the point of the children that a couple conceive…some children appearing more beautiful or handsome than others which can cause jealousy and resentment towards them.

As the scriptures above reveal, "We ourselves also were foolish, disobedient (not loyal towards God), deceived, and serving various lusts and pleasures, living in malice and envy, hateful and hating one another." Thus, no man or woman is found to be without sin in their lives at one time or another. God just picked them up saving them and revitalizing, renewing, and regenerating their souls and spirits with loving kindness, forgiveness, and mercy in the Holy Spirit. Hopefully, they had repented.

And in serving various lusts and pleasures, one needs to evaluate their life and look deeply to possibly see such things bleeding inside and outside ourselves. As a matter of fact, it sometimes takes some people… a spouse, partner, friend or other loved one to point out such weaknesses we have attained within ourselves to finally admit them and work toward elimination of their roots or sources in our lives. And certainly, without the cleansing power of prayer and the Holy Spirit's intervention in such a process… where would we be, but lost in Satan and the world.

Some people may ask, "How will I know if the words of my mouth that I speak are pleasing to the Lord? How then can we submit ourselves unto the Lord in forgiveness of our sins and loyalty to Him? Do we truly believe that we can be forgiven our daily bread for hurt or harm against another in our words and deeds? What then would be some signs or indicators that a blessed cleansing is happening deep inside our hearts and souls towards others?"

Revelation: Some people really have found a connection with the Lord and Holy Spirit appearing on the correct path headed for glory here on earth. Maybe, you can find them in churches, neighborhoods, and communities?

Endeavor: Also, may we allow ourselves forgiveness in breaking away from the lusts, pleasures, hateful attitudes, and malice of the world to become loyal in our fellowship with the Lord.

Prayer: May God's voice reveal the ugly things to us which He knows are causing us individual harm in our lives, thus harming others whom we communicate with and love from our actions, words, and deeds. Let us remember the mercy of the Lord and how He saves us through cleansing, regeneration, and a renewing of the Holy Spirit. Amen.

FEAR THOU NOT

Fear thou not: for I am with thee; be not dismayed; for I am thy God: I will strengthen thee: yea, I will help thee: yea, I will uphold thee with my right hand of righteousness.

ISAIAH 41:1

Our focus for prayer in this entry stems from four areas: Spirit-filled worship service, building a deeper relationship with God, looking for a faith increase, and how can or will our church officers take the lead in all of this? I will intertwine their roles throughout my writing. However, take note, read intently, and know that God is present throughout the wording. All that we can do is to become listening and obedient students of God's word. Open, Spirit-filled, and sanctified in, by, and because of His words and directions for our lives in our loyalty to Him!

First of all saints, we need to come with our minds, bodies, and spirits set on the Lord. We need to come in totally fixed upon the Lord…afraid of nothing, especially God Himself. We need to come in prepared with our Bibles, hymnals and Disciplines (in the AME Church). If we can get them or have them available so that we may readily make reference to them throughout our service as needed. This is especially true, if one is a loyal church officer in helping to lead the congregation in the rituals and traditions of his or her church.

From the very beginning, we should be ready to accept whatever thoughts, feelings, and ways for which the Holy Spirit presents individually to us in our Spirit-filled worship service. Whether it be prostrating ourselves, coming to the altar in prayer, sitting or standing at our seats, and clapping in song with the choir or Praise Team or falling down on our knees. We need to be protected and covered by the ushers and not denied our rightful place amongst the saints in the House of our Lord.

We need not worry about what our family members, fellow saints, or visitors are thinking or doing because we have entered into a Holy place with the Lord where He is opening and welcoming us into His Kingdom, His domain and we need to come faithfully and obediently unto Him in praise and thanksgiving humbly as His loyal children. Certainly, in the Order of service, there can also be a time of testimonials about the love, the perseverance, and the help for which the Lord has given and aided you in by bringing you through a situation(s) which you overcame because of Him. This is where we can help others in the congregation to follow suit and satisfy the wants and needs of the Holy Spirit before God.

In turn, what this does is enable us to build a deeper, stronger, and holier presence and relationship with God as we repent of our own sins, ask forgiveness, and magnify His Holy name in front of the church body who thereby become witnesses to our relationship and the greatness of God, His Son, and the Holy Spirit, thus the power of the Holy Trinity. Most importantly, to know that God is with us, strengthening us, and upholding us in our sacred duties to the church.

Following, such experiences in the life of Christ enable us to evangelize God's word to others outside of His kingdom revealing His goodness, mercy, grace, and forgiveness in our own lives to then want to share with others and allow them the opportunities to experience His greatness as well, thus develop relationships with Christ for their own redemption in the Lord and saving graces. How we are allowed to receive the Holy Spirit really does take priority for how others perceive and receive the Spirit as well in one's sanctuary.

One must not hold back or hinder the Holy Spirit from entering into the service of the saints. Along with this, brings an increase in one's faith...the substance of things hoped for and the evidence of things yet not seen. A Spirit-filled worship service must be pleasing to its hearers most importantly, which is where the work of the church officers all come into play. The ministers, trustees, stewards, and class leaders all play important roles in the edification of the service. That it be to the glory of the Lord as they take the lead in the sanctified service.

Of course, they all need to extend such roles outside of the church as well to be beacons of hope to the lost, forgotten, deserted, and disenfranchised sectors of our communities and bring them into the house of the Lord to be saved! We must not forget that what and how others see us in the church must be the epitome of how others view us from the outside looking in as well. This is not to say that we have never sinned, for we all have fallen short of the glory of God. But we must allow others to see the goodness in what being a follower of Christ can bring to one's life and relationship with Him.

How many of us as parishioners believe that we have a Holy obligation to work in our churches? In other words, if you are voted in or placed by your minister in a position of importance within your church, then will you feel obligated to obey the responsibilities which come with the office? Likewise, as even a member of the congregation... should one feel an allegiance to one's congregation to serve say in the capacity of a choir member, usher and so forth as part of your Christian journey and fulfillment unto the Lord?

Revelation: In our getting understanding of Christ's Holiness, may we remain loyal to Him as His faithful servants here on earth.

Endeavor: We know that we have the wherewithal to do mighty things in our churches according to God's word such as forming Christian relationships, bringing others to Christ, and tithing of our incomes to the Lord.

Prayer: Help us, Heavenly Father, to become Your great servants to reach the masses of lost souls and to become the stewards of faith for others to witness in their devotional spaces at church. Let us not be critical of those being converted in Your word but act as saints saved by God's grace to then bring others into God's fold. Amen.

MARRIAGE

(The Institution whereby
Individuals are Joined Together)

COVENANT KISS

So, ought men to love their wives as their own bodies.
He that loveth his wife loveth himself. For no man
ever yet hateth his own flesh; but nourisheth and
cherisheth it, even as the Lord the church.

EPHESIANS 5:28-29

My husband and I married almost nineteen years ago and have had our share of challenges, both positive and negative. Sadly, much of our concentration has dealt with health issues on both sides. Unfortunately for us both, we have had to endure both his life's story and equally, mine in family health histories. Several of which have finally caught up with us as we have been allowed to grow gracefully in our ages and marital challenges.

There were times when we'd wondered if and when such diagnoses were going to end or just prolong their gravity in our lives. And to that end, much of our health is dependent upon the wholistic lifestyles which we choose to follow. Through it all, we have been faithful, loving, obedient, and supportive one toward the other just as God has mandated for a fruitful and thriving marital union in covenant with Him. Thus, we pray and study the Bible (words) of God together.

My husband has generally put my needs ahead of his own as I have likewise done. There have been times when we had to take time-outs and reevaluate our current marital status wholistically...from physical, mental, and social viewpoints. We had to validate the situations which we encountered on both a short-term and long-term basis. If changes deemed necessary, sometimes with and sometimes without hesitation… we made them.

We came into our marriage from previous relationships and marriages so we indeed had a lot invested into our marital covenant. First and most importantly, stood our relationship with God, our Father. My present husband had coincidentally been the spiritual leader for my first husband and myself, also a Bible School and Sunday School teacher during that union so, we knew that he was centered on the promises of God as I was first and foremost.

Therefore, coming into our union, I knew that my current husband and I had held God to a higher standard than had some of our family, friends and acquaintances prior to our marriage. Losing some relationships just plain hurt but we knew they had to go for what we were working hard to achieve in God's grace. So, we let them go and have not had any regrets centered in God.

Happily, one day my husband had struggled with previous knee problems and subsequent surgeries on the same knee again that now, the fifth surgery must have been the charm! I remember that my best friend whom I call my sister and best friend and her fiancé had come down to the hospital to take me out for lunch and more importantly, be present to greet my husband with me once he came out of recovery. Thus, there we sat upon his arrival to his room!

I'll never forget seeing him in his hospital bed as he had just been wheeled in moments before our arrival. I was just so excited that he had made it through another surgery and was looking really well! Upon seeing him I drew closely to his bedside as he lifted his head and we shared a very special covenant kiss as my sister-friend who cried crocodile tears nicknamed it. She had felt that she had witnessed what was such a strong conviction of the love and commitment which we shared between each other and knew that it couldn't have been anything less than of God.

Therefore, as stated above each man who loves his wife as his own body thus, loves himself. Likewise, he should love and cherish his body. I would say that the same scriptures apply to the woman equally. To me, these words seal the covenant of the relationship given by God. I do believe that my dear sister friend was witness to something truly sanctified by the Lord that day and was allowed to then transfer her thoughts and feelings thereafter to me. I was truly humbled and grateful.

However, thinking on marriages, how often do we lose sight of the love we should openly share with our marital partner? Do we praise God for the love we are able to share together? Do we continue to nourish and cherish our love between each other as we grow in God's marital covenant? Or do we just continue to take one another for granted despite the gift which God has given us?

Revelation: Help us to be forever present to our soulmate whom God has joined together.

Endeavor: Despite our differences, may we stay united with our covenant kiss in Christ daily.

Prayer: Allow us to renew our covenant vows with the Lord as needed. Allow us to be a beacon of hope, life, and Christianity for those who are witnesses to our union. May we help others to find Your love in their own relationships as we remain doers of Your word. Amen.

SMALL SIPS OF TEA

And the king loved Esther above all the women, and she obtained grace and favor in his sight more than all the virgins; so that he set the royal crown upon her head, and made her queen instead of Vashti.

ESTHER 2:17

What a tall order it seemed that King Ahasuerus had in replacing his wife, Queen Vashti. As the Bible states, Queen Esther was certainly not the king's first choice of mate and Vashti was not one that took umbrage to actions of the king either.

As the story goes, King Ahasuerus held a grandiose feast fit for a king in the court of the palace. Women were not invited to the festivities; only men. She did however, host a feast for the women concubines who lived in the king's estate. They probably drank small sips of tea as they shared womanly talk and conversed about the state of affairs with the outside festivities and the king.

King Ahasuerus became like a party animal and partied for days and nights for a week in front of his chamberlains (advisers), princes, and noblemen; both rich and poor men from over a hundred and seven and twenty provinces after the third year of his reign from India to Ethiopia.

Literally, they did not stop for a week drinking wine and feasting on the legs of lamb and best cooked foods to be found in the provinces. Finally, on the Sabbath Day when the king was drunken with wine, he sent his chamberlains to fetch Queen Vashti and bring her forth to him the king. It was his goal to let them parade her dazzling beauty before the congregation of men as well as his vanity for such a possession.

Vashti refuses to enter the King's presence and follow his commandment which makes him froth at the mouth as he grows so angry and is feeling totally humiliated in front of his princes in the court. Talking with them, they decide that something major has to happen to Queen Vashti who has set a precedent among women to not obey and be disrespectful toward their husbands and thus result in much contempt and wrath in the marital union.

They finally conclude that Queen Vashti has to become dethroned and banished from the palace altogether. They allow King Ahasuerus to find and select a new queen to embody the estate and take her throne in the plan of action taking over four years spanning Persia and Media. Finally, the King then chooses Esther amongst all of the virgins he had bedded to become his queen replacing Vashti.

Not until that time frame and sequence of events, did King Ahasuerus find Esther and bestow the royal crown upon her head. It was not because of Vashti not getting the crown that Esther became queen. She previously had worn it, earned it and reigned as queen.

Just how many women would have disobeyed their mate's words to go out and adorn yourself amongst this unknown group of men that Vashti was to be paraded in front of? How many feel that Vashti was justified by the Lord for the stance which she chose to take against her husband? And if it were you in Vashti's position, how many women believe that receiving a crown was worth what Vashti was being asked to do for her husband?

Revelation: We have to stand up to our beliefs and values rooted in God.

Endeavor: Speak firm about knowing and doing right from wrong as many may be affected in your decision.

Prayer: Even when the world stands against our values and beliefs, we need to voice that God has our back, possibly over small sips of tea which can calm our spirits. Lead us into the truth of a matter; not a falsity in history as nothing is just handed to us but with diligence and hard work... we win the prize which is self-esteem and pride in the matter. Amen.

THE ODD COUPLE

*And I will bless her, and give thee a son also of her:
yea, I will bless her, and she shall be a mother of
nations; kings of people shall be of her. Then Abraham
fell upon his face, and laughed, and said in his heart,
Shall a child be born unto him that is a hundred years
old? And shall Sarah, that is ninety years old, bear?*

GENESIS 17:16-17

The words of God were bonified, but most importantly, sanctified accordingly. Anything that He professed and said would become a reality into existence, did just that. Time and time again, God Himself, mystified and glorified those of His flock to the point of building covenants with nations and men working miracles right before their eyes. God even changed his people's names to carry through with the tasks He yet had before them to conquer.

One couple in particular, renamed Abraham and Sarah by God was one of great significance and oddity in nature. They were well aged and I am sure were filled with wisdom, grace, faith, and hope in their days. Abraham was almost one hundred and Sarah was ninety years old. I feel quite certain that they lived by the rules of their land, religion, and culture. Most importantly, they had both believed in God the Father and the sanctity of marriage and parenthood.

As it were, God had blessed Abraham when he was known as Abram to take another wife, through the recommendation and blessing of his wife Sarai at the time. Sarai knew that she was barren after so many of her years and knew that there was no way in which she could produce an heir for her husband who greatly yearned such. Therefore, she made a decision of great sacrifice for her husband.

Their plan was for Hagar to become impregnated and bear Abram a child. In particular, it was a son and they would name him, Ishmael to then be instructed and trained to carry on the affairs and lineage of Abram. And of course, such a birth allowed Abram the status of fatherhood and a male heir to carry on God's messages and covenant unto his people and nations. I wonder if his birth made Abraham feel fulfilled in the eyes of the Lord, let alone in his manhood?

To get back to the oddity in their relationship between Sarah and Abraham, God made a decision to place them above the scrutiny of mankind and bless them in a way that did not even seem feasible in their elder ages. He told Abraham that Sarah would bear him a son and that his name shall be called Isaac. Sarah would be a mother of nations and kings of people shall be of her. God would establish a covenant with Isaac and the seed (heirs) after him.

Can you imagine being on the receiving end of the message from God Himself? Would you have fallen into shock, disbelief, and laughed as it is written that Abraham did upon falling on his face before God. Or would one just accept the message which was given him or her and go about one's regular business based on knowing and believing upon the promises of God that all things can become possible and fulfilled according to His word? And what about Sarah, all the changes which she as an aged woman possibly had to endure to even get through the pregnancy and birth?

Revelation: The most seemingly, supernatural events can occur in one's lifetime today as it was revealed and written in the past.

Endeavor: May we find ways to look at the bigger pictures found in all situations, even those which seem different or odd beyond our understanding at such times to find God has been in it all along.

Prayer: Enable us as Your people to believe in Your word to the point of miraculous encounters as we Your children witness to miracles all around us in our daily life. Let us not laugh and think that what we have heard from God is a spoof but rather believe it is destined to manifest physically in our lives. Amen.

RIGHTEOUS LIVING

And they were both righteous before God, walking in all the commandments and ordinances of the Lord blameless. And they had no child, because that Elisabeth was barren, and they both were now well stricken in years.

ST. LUKE 1:6-7

Walking blameless and shameless before the Lord following all of His commandments and laws were Zechariah, a priest of the Abijah lineage and Elisabeth, a daughter of Aaron. They were married and both were of advanced ages acting I'm sure as sanctified agents of God and change to come unbeknown to them for generations of time.

Probably in their quaint country of Judea, despite King Herod and all of his rules to live by in governing men and their families, both Zechariah and Elisabeth were sought out by townspeople because of their abiding faith, loving dispositions, and righteous living for God.

One day while Zechariah was burning incense in God's temple so that he could pray, he sensed a presence near his side which was the angel of the Lord, Gabriel. This totally confused and scared him to the point of probably falling to his knees in worship to God to be held blameless before men and the Lord.

Gabriel tried to reassure Zechariah that all was alright and he had merely been sent by the Father to give him a message. It seemed that Zechariah had always prayed to God throughout the years that Elisabeth would birth him a son. Finally, they'd be parents after all of these years.

Suddenly, such a prayer would become a reality as revealed by Gabriel to Zechariah and that he should be named John. He would be one free of wine and intoxicating drinks filled with the Holy Ghost which would come over him as he leaped in his mother, Elisabeth's womb. This happened when Mary visited her cousin and told her of Jesus' impending birth. John would endeavor to be like the prophet, Elijah to the people of Israel spreading God's word and bringing the disobedient children into God's fold.

How many of us would have been faithful enough and righteous enough to have been chosen such as Elisabeth to bear children at her age? Random conceptions and births are happening to women in advanced ages today. But, to have been able to have one's conception announced by an angel of God was a really big deal for a ninety-year-old woman! Truly, a faith walk in obedience wouldn't one say?

Revelation: Make us do a checkpoint to see if we are living righteously according to God.

Endeavor: How many of us would be ready to receive a word, let alone a gift of a baby from the Lord no matter the messenger or the message?

Prayer: Help direct us to Your commandments in times of discernment from the messenger. Remind us that You are the Lord and all final decisions come and are from You. What we think may be impossible, God says is possible as we can do all things through Him who strengthens us despite the dissenters. Amen.

ONE NAME ONLY

And the angel said unto her, Fear not, Mary: for thou hast
found favor with God. And behold, thou shalt conceive in thy
womb, and bring forth a son, and shalt call his name JESUS.

ST. LUKE 1:30-31

Mary was known in her community of Nazareth, a city of Galilee as a
woman of God. A virgin, she was betrothed to marry Joseph from the
house of David. It was then in the sixth month that Gabriel, an angel
was sent by Mary's side with a message from God. "Hail, thou art highly
favored, the Lord is with thee: blessed art thou amongst women." St.
Luke 1:28.

Afterwards, Mary began feeling very uncomfortable quite possibly
by his announcement because she was selected over other young women
her age and for what manner of a task was she to perform? I can only
speculate as to what level of ambivalence she had attained at this most
critical moment but it seems like it took her a little while before she
could perceive what was happening around and to her. Possibly, she felt
less than worthy to have been so exalted? Better yet, what words might
Joseph think or feel if he knew of Gabriel's message? She was simply
stated, a young woman ready to marry the man of her dreams. How
dare anything or anyone change that fact but God? Their life choices
laid ahead of them as they had probably talked about and planned time
and time again.

Soon after, the angel told Mary the message which God wanted
her to hear but not out of fear. He was not there to frighten her. He

was there to put the love of Christ before her and quite quickly. I am sure that Gabriel tried to calm her with his words from the Lord that soon she would become with child but not by her promised Joseph as her husband. Instead, Mary who had no previous sexual relations with him would become overshadowed by the power of the Lord working with the Holy Ghost and a son would be born called one name only... JESUS!

I cannot even imagine the thoughts which were racing through Mary's mind concerning all that she had heard and needed to prepare herself for. With the biggest challenge being her allegiance to Joseph and no other man, she had unchartered territory to inhabit as the chosen mother of our Lord, JESUS. What a feat for someone so young and pure yet again, exalted and found highly favored by the Lord amongst all women.

How many of us could even step into the feet of Mary who had never been with her husband to be, Joseph? Would it have been enough to just listen to the angel and begin to believe, let alone bear a birth of such magnitude to mankind? Exactly how did she get through those nine months of pregnancy with her family and friends? Do you think that she ever felt shame in any of this or that the angel, Gabriel calmed her nerves, fears, and anxieties...if she suffered any of them? After all, the angel came to not only announce the word of God but calm her spirit as well in preparation for all that was to befall she and Joseph from conception to delivery of baby JESUS.

Revelation: We can be ready to listen for the message which God sends to our ears, minds, and hearts without fear.

Endeavor: Let us forever call His name Jesus, the great Son's name daily.

Prayer: Thank you, Lord, for having found favor in Mary to exalt her as mother of our Savior, Jesus Christ. Also, for those of us who have felt your excitation and deliverance in a matter, we know that You don't bring us to a place and leave us. Rather, You weave and mold us into those beings that You want us to be to celebrate Your name and your Son, Jesus. Amen.

UNEARNED FAVOR

And the Lord God caused a deep sleep to fall upon Adam, and
he slept; and he took one of his ribs, and closed up the flesh
instead thereof; And the rib, which the Lord God had taken from
man, made he a woman, and brought her unto the man. And
Adam said, This is now bone of my bones, and flesh of my flesh:
she shall be called Woman, because she was taken out of Man.

GENESIS 2: 21-23

And so, mankind was fulfilled with the making of woman, man's
helpmate. It seems so amazing to read or listen to the making or creation
of man, but especially woman. God took a rib from her male companion
and soulmate, Adam and placed it into the very being, body of Eve
making them bone upon bone and flesh upon flesh one to another in
our God's name.

Our Lord God had now begun His destination for our father and
mother known to humankind called unearned favor for which they had
been predestined to fulfill in this life cycle of man and woman. They
literally stood naked looking at one another in the Garden of Eden
having no shame and why should they? There was no guilt or shame
to speak of.

They hadn't violated any laws or rules governing them or the fowl
of the air, cattle of the earth, amphibians, reptiles, or aqua marine life
of the waters. Our Lord God had created everything upon this earth
including the heavens and earth, night and day, peace and tumults,
vegetables and fruit trees to be harvested and all of the multiplicities in

between. All of this as a gift given to Adam and Eve bestowed upon them in love, obedience, and trust over the things on and in the earth and waters from our Lord God.

God did need not test their loyalty or obedience to earn such recognizable favor. But rather invested in their countenance and actions to demonstrate such vestiges above in His creation. There were no other human witnesses to the good which they displayed towards one another, the earth or God either directly or indirectly.

Therefore, one can easily deduce that no angel was sent forth from God to give Adam and Eve their good news of unearned favor. Rather, it was stated directly by the Lord to them both. Adam even had been given total control over the naming of all other creatures on the earth and they could use or work with them at their discretion. They had absolute power like a king and queen to reign over their kingdom or sovereignty.

One might ask, "What made them so special that God blessed them so abundantly?" Remember, they were the first man and woman created. Probably, this is why God then chose Adam and Eve and no one else to bestow His unearned favor. Is unearned favor still given upon family members today as a birthright? Have any readers out there ever been given unearned favor in his or her lifetime? Why do you think it was given to you and do you think that you have an obligation within your household, neighborhood or community to give back something of yourself in words, actions, or deeds?

Revelation: May we resolve to do the needed good work on earth for our Lord God.

Endeavor: Hopefully, we humans here on earth can be exalted in our marriages according to our Lord God based on His favor for our lives.

Prayer: Help us to show favor one toward another in our Lord God's name as we fully commit and abide in the words of the Bible and God's commandments as we learn daily the blessings of our Father in heaven. If we are unchurched, enable us to fellowship in a church which we might soon call home to learn what God's favor can do in marriages and the life of the family. Amen.

AS MY SOUL DREAMS ON ANGELS' WINGS

As my soul dreams...
I am comforted and delighted smiling in my slumber
     hearing sounds of sweet, child-like laughter resonate
          from angels descending from their Heavenly gates above.

Gaily, they hurriedly surround me as I sense
     their gloriously, spread wings of loving
          warmth, radiant brilliance, and majestic grandeur.

Paradoxically, and without forewarning a door mysteriously
     opens releasing three, great, and foreboding shadows that
          study me while harboring threats of despair, harm and death.

As my soul dreams...
I feel overwhelmed by the magnitude of this situation as the
     presence of these shadows waits intrepidly for an opening
          to penetrate through God's protective wall for my life.

With fury burning incessantly,
     these pestilent shadows simply merge as one
     now targeting the core of my very soul!

Desperately, they search for a snare
     to break through our Lord God's plan
          for my servitude on this Earth!

As my soul dreams ...
I am left falling deeper and deeper
into an unrecognizable frenzy disconnecting me
to my reality until I become hastily awakened!

With my eyes now opened to my spiritual nakedness,
I recognize these bizarre and haunting shadows as
demonic militia allowed to dwell within my soul.

Glimpsing hazily from my mind's eye,
I catch reflections of my life's story filled
with its many, illusive and superfluous faces.

Having endured sufferings from multiple struggles and crippling
falsehoods,
has yielded self-imposed fears, malignantly-fed disappointments,
and far too many exhaustive and lost opportunities.

As my soul dreams...
I relinquish self to such dauntless shadows which
have borne piercing crucifixes and crushing vexations
lodged between my bones and flesh and breathed unto
my spirit.

Physically manifesting themselves as injurious assaults against my body,
these shadows rapidly descend like vultures unto their prey,
swooping down with their talons to rip my soul apart!

Developing sweltering, heart palpitations and menacing, cold sweats,
my heart feels like it will jump right out of my body until
quite abruptly, the shadows... simply flee from me!

As my soul dreams...
Upon hearing the same door mysteriously slam shut,
my eyes miraculously become opened to my soul's own truth
left lying helplessly in perspiration and soiled clothing.

Submerged in inextinguishable guilt sobbing uncontrollably,
  I resolve to take full acceptance of my own wretchedness
    now eating through its invasion of my tormented spirit.

Willfully surrendering my soul unto Jesus,
  I witness the awesomeness of God's most eminent angels
    begin to commence their utterings in child-like laughter
    again.

Gently, and uniformly as they begin casting down
  their army's grand fortress that surrounds me...
    before their ascension back unto the Heavens above!

Joyously, intoxicated and spiritually filled,
  my soul unleashes voluminous tears that stream down my face...
    cleansing and comforting my anointed spirit through
    song.

As my soul dreams...
"Mine eyes have seen the glory of the coming of the Lord..."
  with His magnificent, saving graces and His bountiful, tender
    mercies along my spiritual pilgrimage on angels' wings!

Written by Donna Collier Rickman

OBEDIENCE

(Submissive to the restraint
or command of authority)

LISTENING INTENTLY

Therefore, my beloved brethren, let every man be swift
to hear, slow to speak, slow to wrath; for the wrath of
man does not produce the righteousness of God.

JAMES 1:19, 20

Growing up in Sunday School during the sixties seemed like years
ago, but us young ones learned the voices, mannerisms, and the body
language of our most beloved elders just the same. I can remember that
on this one particular occasion, some of us kids got to talking loudly
about leaving church. Even though we were signaled by our elders with
piercing eyes, flickering eyeballs, and disapproving body language,
like usual we'd sneak out anyway to make our way down the street and
around the corner to our local A & P store.

On this one particular morning, I couldn't decide between two
candies to buy and meant to put the one back on the shelf, but hadn't.
I had it in my other hand when the store official accused me of
shoplifting. To top it off who walks in the store, but my father looking
right at me at the counter. Luckily, I was not cited for any shoplifting
but received another message from my father that was unspoken yet
revealed at the same time upon his face. Get ready for when I hit the
door at home!

He had gotten word through the elders upon entering church that
a group of us had gone. Surprisingly, he was pretty quiet when we left
the store. Thinking back, it was actually during the silence on the drive
home after church that I felt the presence of God at my side. Listening

intently for what He had to say, helped quench my need for deliverance from my impending doom which awaited me momentarily.

It was if God knew my every qualm and fear from that moment on. He told me to remain calm, not crying erratically or profusely and trying to apologize for something I had not committed...especially any shoplifting. So, just chill. Hopefully, your father will calm down and realize the truth in those last moments at the store when I didn't get charged after all. Most importantly, God forgave me for any disobedience toward my elders and I thanked Him.

In any event, I heeded God's righteousness and forgiveness always remembering Daddy's full wrath felt on his belt after we got home. Quiet, yet deadly was his motto! Do we sometimes forget the abundance of wit and wisdom assured us from our elders? Have we forgotten to revel upon them as such beacons in our lives? Can we or will we, someday be looked upon and held up in ways that our elders were when we were growing up leading towards righteousness?

Revelation: We must not forget our moral values bestowed upon us from our elders.

Endeavor: Let us forever stay focused on You, Lord, to do Your will no matter Your wrath.

Prayer: Help us, Lord, to remember to listen and remain obedient to those important people in our lives who mean only well in our youthfulness. Help us also from whence our Christian moral teachings came from, enable us to do the same for other youth and our own grandchildren as they age and mature in their daily lives. Thus, we as adults will become swift to hear but slow to speak and show wrath toward them. Amen.

WHISPERING RAINDROPS

"If you walk in my statues and keep my commandments, and perform them, then I will give you rain in its season, the land shall yield to produce, and the trees of the field shall yield their fruit."

LEVITICUS 26:3-4 (NKJV)

Can't you hear the water falling…gently whispering raindrop to raindrop to perform their miracles of watering and nurturing our bodies, animals, vegetations, and environments from your locale to the farthest destinations in the world? Every living thing should be so blessed!

Just think about the job of rain in its seasons; allowing trees to yield their fruits and lands to produce harvests. What would we do without water? How might we survive and for how long without the nurturing and nutritional values of water found within the vegetables and fruits which we eat and thrive? Let alone, the amount of water found within our human bodies to function daily.

According to The National Health and Medical Research Council (Ministry of Health in the Australian Government), "Water is defined as an essential nutrient because it is required in amounts that exceed the body's ability to produce it." And even though we know that water constitutes over 70% of green plants, they still need extra, supplemental water to grow strong, reproduce and sustain life as well.

All of this is given from the Lord above as we obey and follow His statutes and His ten commandments according to the Bible. That's a tall order as a Christian to follow, but one which separates us from the non-believer in Christ Jesus, His Father and the Holy Spirit as we listen and obey as the Lord will provide us with needed rain and water in due seasons.

Is it then up to us to decide to follow God's lead to make for a fuller and more abundant life throughout our journey on earth. How can we not follow the commandments and walk in God's statutes as His disciples today? Just how often do you have a little talk with God to make everything all right? And in our faults, do we learn to correct what is wrong for an abundant and fruitful life in the Lord?

Revelation: Yield not unto temptation away from God's commandments.

Endeavor: Let us learn to value the importance of water in our daily lives and the lives of other creatures, great and small as well as our vegetations.

Prayer: Father, help us to follow and implement Your words of obedience for abundant living. For even in a mustard seed, You bring forth newness of life and living for us to witness. Let us become great servants of Your will on and in this earth of land, waters, and skies which You have gifted us to use wisely for our benefit. Amen.

BLESSED SERVANT OF GOD

And Deborah, a prophetess, the wife of Lapidot, she judged Israel at that time. And she dwelt under the palm tree of Deborah between Ramah and Bethel in mount Ephraim and the children of Israel came up to her for judgement. And she sent and called Barak the son of Abinoam out of Kedeshnaphtali, and said unto him, Hath not the Lord God of Israel commanded, saying, Go and draw toward mount Tabor and take with thee ten thousand men of the children of Naphtali and of the children of Zebulun?

JUDGES 4:4-6

Deborah, a Biblical prophetess, was an individual highly thought of as being in contact with God and speaking on His behalf as she received public and/or private messages from Him. She was the only female judge noted in the Bible, having served from 1107 BC. until her death in 1067 BC. She also was a poet, songwriter, songstress, and warrior who summoned Barack to battle against an army of invaders as she tarried along with him. Afterwards, she wrote a victory song of poetry in Judges 5 as her story was first told in prose in Judges 4.

I wonder, were women for or against Deborah at that time? Firstly, to earn the title of judgeship in itself was an unbelievable feat for a woman during those times...let alone a man. To think of what she must have endured from societal, class, and gender role, clashes, and conflicts in public scrutiny themselves makes her industrious to journey into such isolated territory, remarkable to say the least as she was also a wife. Her husband must have had no problem in pulling up his own breaches in such a male-dominated system resisting a women's rights movement.

Secondly, had she been a mother also or unable to bear any children? Or did she somehow avoid pregnancy? The research which I have found does not make any mention of her motherhood. However, the amount of stress placed upon her during those times had to fill up a whole big pot of worries taking up most of her time. Where would mothering have come into the picture even with the help of servants or family members as today, women have their choices in daycares and schools for their children to attend.

Thirdly, and most importantly, we cannot dismiss this call which she had as a warrior of God listening for His voice to direct her thoughts, decisions, actions, and steps into war was by far miraculous, that she would advance her missions accordingly answering to God. How strategic and effective such directives must have been in her obedience to be alert and focused on the tasks at hand... let alone her judicial duties which were front and center over the Israelites.

Fourthly, with all of the gifts, talents, strength, and power which she had been blessed by from the Lord with to use as needed, it is a wonder that such a delicate flower (poet, writer, songstress) could also blossom to that of destroyer, judge, and jury. I wonder had the Israelite people elevated, adored, and adorned her in such the latter positions or was she thought of as a sort of oddball...out of place at the time within her reign? It seems that God's hands held her protecting her from all hurt, harm, and danger no matter her challenges in her life. Truly, Deborah was inspired by God and worked obediently through the power of the Holy Spirit to deliver personal messages to her Israelite people.

According to the Bible, Deborah had the challenge of making judgeship over Jabin, the king of Canaan that reigned in Hazor whose host was Sisera for which he oppressed the children for twenty years. Under her palm tree is where she made judgements for her people. I wonder... what significance did such a tree provide for Deborah? Was it someplace that she heard from the Lord in making her judgements to then feed into the making of the verdicts? What can we conclude based on the information at hand for what it takes to hear from God and in what locality?

Certainly, most of us cannot attest to being a prophet or prophetess as Deborah but know in fact, that we received a word from God...a message to be shared amongst His people here on earth as we are indeed His blessed servants. Do most of us dig deeper to find resolve about the steps and guidance we are to draw from and put into action, or do we just ignore what has been reverently brought forth to our eyes and ears to manifest and do? Lastly, how can we listen to know the words were from God? Do we take time to pray over them and ask God for His blessings and discernment to go forth and act?

Revelation: It may be true that we are not all prophets or prophetesses, however God can and does knowingly speak to us to do His will on earth.

Endeavor: Can we as women draw strength from the service of Deborah to lead and share our special gifts and talents in our communities to serve God?

Prayer: May we especially as women learn to open up our spirits to you oh Lord, in being Your obedient servants. Knowing that we as human beings have a mighty way to go in listening for Your words and will... versus our own to be prosperous and God-fearing such as Deborah despite her challenges Amen.

BLESSINGS FOREVERMORE

Do all things without murmurings and disputings: That ye may be blameless and harmless, the sons of God, without rebuke, in the midst of a crooked and perverse nation, among whom ye shine as lights in the world.

PHILIPPIANS 2:14, 15

When was the last time you voluntarily gave of yourself to a worthy cause or effort? One in which you acted as part of a team, willing and able to offer your services free of charge with no thought of recompense, murmurings and disputing amongst your teammates? Able to renounce the devil and freely uphold the righteousness of God as you endeavored to proclaim His word and perform His works giving all glory to Him and not to the powers of wickedness in the world.

The Bible states, "Know that I am God and worthy to be praised." "Be still and know that I am God; I will be exalted among the nations, I will be exalted in the earth." Psalm 46:10 Therefore, despite all of the uncertainty, crookedness and perversity in the nation; God still reigns as King over all nations. We should be ready wear our armor of protection for the Lord, especially in the ways in which we talk and behave as others are forever watching us.

How often are we witnesses to the sins of the world but not cloaked in our right minds? Not giving praises to our Father in Heaven for all of the good and sanctity of a nation which we observe in our daily interactions and workings despite the negative people and works which we encounter. Still, we should be forever mindful of the good which dwells in most of us because of the beauty, power, and grace of the Lord as it is Him who keeps us.

So, in spite of any and all murmurings and disputing by others, we purposely should place ourselves at a different level, high above all the negativity which surrounds us in our daily living. In all of our tasks; let us do them out of obedience and to the delight of our Lord. No need to sulk in self-pity or disobedience so that we may be seen as blameless and harmless as the sons and daughters of God.

Oh, give thanks you sons and daughters of God for all of His marvelous works in the world as His light shines ever so brightly with blessings forevermore remembering that salvation is our final prize to victory in discipleship. Not the opposite, loathing in the devil's footsteps and following his ways and doing his dirt as he roams the earth causing havoc wherever he goes.

Who reigns in all of the muck and mire? If we must ask, we must also remember this: "Who is it that we follow and by what measure can we be held blameless and harmless in the lightness of day or the darkness of night?" We must ask ourselves in the crevices of our hearts, bodies, and souls…what would God have us to do in light of everything else and how should our tasks and living be done? Certainly, not in vain.

Revelation: Be a team player and renounce the devil to proclaim the righteousness of God.

Endeavor: Let our lights shine with blessings forevermore in the Lord.

Prayer: Help us remember that You are God and worthy to be praised. No amount of disarray and negativity in our thoughts and actions should go unheard from You as we must remember to stay focused on you Lord and stay in perfect peace. Amen.

BE AT ATTENTION

For I am persuaded, that neither death, nor life, nor
angels, nor principalities, nor powers, or things present,
nor things to come, Nor height, nor depth, or any
other creature, shall be able to separate us from the
love of God, which is in Christ Jesus our Lord.

ROMANS 8:38 -39

It seems that to become persuaded means to be convinced without any shadow of doubt of the vast amount of love for which Christ Jesus our Lord has for all of His children to thus, make us be at attention of such omnipresence and omnipotence here on earth. Allow our Father to use us as His vessels of communication and salvation for our lost brothers and sisters.

In times like these, we need a Savior, that is for sure, that allows the Spirit to make intercession for us all! With all that has proceeded us in history, and is unlike our current conditions in the world...Lord, please save us from all of our iniquities. Please allow us not to be separated from that Great Love which is found in You.

When the above scriptures were spoken, they were told by Paul, an apostle of Jesus. Paul was talking to the Roman church about their salvation. That nothing, no matter how minute or grand could ever split them from our Lord. Whether death, life, angels, principalities, powers, present or future things, height, depth, or any other creature. Think on these words for how majestic, valiant and filled with grandeur that they were and are.

Fall on your knees and prostrate your whole being before the Lord in pure submission and holiness for the love of our Father. Imagine, coming before our Lord. Who could even begin to lift one's eyes and look upon His radiance, grace, and mercy which He has given to us freely despite any disobedience and distrust in Him?

Everything which He hath created is somehow mentioned in one way or another in these two versus as there is nothing new under the sun that He does not know. Therefore, any fears, phobias, anxiousness, shame, disabilities, shortcomings, or insecurities, through the love of Christ, our Lord and the power of the Holy Spirit as intercessor; we shall be set free as conquerors and not be caught up in the fray.

We simply need to humble ourselves and give all honor and glory to God our Father and listen to His teachings as written in the Bible. Because to know Him is to love Him and never allow anyone or anything to overtake us to the point of denial or separation from Him and His protection, guidance, and undying love.

Can't you feel it my sister or brother, when someone or something threatens to break up that relationship which you have with our Father? In times like that, what do you do? Do you blow it off or hold steadfast to the promises for which our Father has for us with Him? How often do you think upon the scriptures above in your daily walk with Him? I beg you to do a check-in daily to see if in fact, a separation has occurred. If so, think on these things and then ask the Holy Spirit for help to mend.

Revelation: Let us be open to re-evaluation by the Holy Spirit interceding on our behalf.

Endeavor: May we be as Paul on a movement to keep us in relationship with our Heavenly Father.

Prayer: Please embolden us with the Holy Spirit's power to be at attention and obedience to the deeds and commands of the Lord. Let us be cognizant of all of God's words that we have grown familiar with through the reading of His words in our daily meditations and prayers while listening for a word or words from our Father. Amen.

SMILE WHEN YOU'RE HAPPY!

Praise ye the Lord, O give thanks unto the Lord; for
He is good: for His mercy endureth forever.

PSALM 106: 1

For each and every day of life, one should give praises to the Lord thanking him for His many wonders, joys, care, enlightenment, forgiveness, inspiration, love, and mercy as they endure forever. In this endeavor, one should smile or laugh knowing that God most certainly has our back and has given favor to each of us in our daily journeys and travails. We should strive to become humble in our relationship with the Father, our Lord and gracious in our affects towards others for He is good and His mercy endures forever. And for this, we should be glad not just for ourselves but for others to share in God's greatness.

During our daily interactions with family and friends, we need to possibly dig deeper into our hearts to smile even when we are unhappy no matter the circumstances because all around us, we are witnessing rampant negativity, cruelty, abuses, and unhappiness within the world and others. God has placed gladness upon our hearts to marvel and relish our moments here on earth as time is precious and carries great weight in terms of fleeting moments. What we witness and cherish in one moment, can perish in the next. So, we should learn to accept such moments for what they are and praise the Lord for them.

He has given us the capacity of free-will to do and respond to life and its circumstances as we so choose. It is like we can choose life or death. Likewise, we can choose to praise and thank God or reject His salvation for our lives and not follow Him. Certainly, He would rather we choose the latter. This is what His plan was about in allowing His Son, Jesus to die on the cross for our sins that we would have everlasting life with it being in Him. Never in our lives will there be anything higher or more worthy to die for.

Again, we should be happy and praise the Lord! I cannot say it enough for if we think about all of the ways in which God has truly blessed us whether we deserved it or not, we should forever be thankful. There have been songs written and sung about being happy such as "If You're Happy and You Know It" by Lil' Baby Bone or "Happy" by Pharrell Williams and other artists who rock our world by being happy and singing happy songs. Just think for a moment of how those songs make us feel in our hearts down into the core of our souls. That's how we should show our willingness to be obedient and praise our Lord.

Think about it, when was the last time you gave praises to the Lord for your life and those of your loved ones? Have you witnessed others such as your family, friends, acquaintances, or even strangers give praises to our Father above? Exactly, what do you witness? Are they singing or crying or falling to the ground? Do they have outstretched arms and hands toward the heavens? Are they sometimes seeming listless, consumed and caught up in another time or place keeping up another pace? Have they taken steps forward as if being moved to another place or step in time with the beats of happiness felt inside?

Or are they more gracious, whereby they possibly smile at the mouth and speak in small words of admiration for the Lord ? In any event, take the time and observe your circle or world in which you live and dwell to see the smiles on people's faces and the praises in general for living on this plane. They could have the love of Christ in their hearts and become a beacon of hope for you and others to believe as well and become obedient to God's will. Leave hardened hearts behind and smile when you're happy!

Revelation: Let us think of the goodness of the Lord as He touches our hearts and souls in mercy forever as we smile in joy and happiness to Him.

Endeavor: May we remember what Jesus did for the world and give praises to the Lord for His goodness in making us obedient to His words.

Prayer: Remind us, Lord, to smile when we're happy and possibly touch someone else's life by praising You. Even at times when sadness and disappointments come upon us, help us to remember the gladness upon which we felt was something renewing and invigorating to our bodies and minds. Amen.

PATIENCE

(Bearing pains or trials calmly
or without any complaint)

PATIENT FAVOR

My brother, count it all joy when ye fall into divers (various)
temptations; knowing this, that the trying of your faith
worketh patience. But let patience have her perfect work,
that ye may be perfect and entire, wanting nothing.

JAMES 1:2-4

Throughout my life, unfortunately I have undergone around fifteen surgical operations/medical procedures between the years of 1978 to 2014. Most have dealt with childbirth or the reproductive and gastrointestinal tract body systems. Others have dealt with biopsies, some were infections, or a specific organ or other body part that simply couldn't adequately function without some needed major repair. In any event, I graduated and made it through all steps and stages as required. Thank God, because there were multiple times in which I wasn't exactly sure of my demise or current state of physical and mental health to actually survive through all the processes including healing and recovery.

One might then ask, "Have I learned how to exemplify patience as a patient (whether as an inpatient or outpatient)?" I can honestly answer, "Yes, I have learned all of that and some in medical practicality, efficiency, and effectiveness as a humble patient!" Generally, I have abided by all of the rules of the pre-surgical preparation partaking in the cleansing of body parts and robing into my hospital garb, following the embedded rules of the ward or isolated seclusions in a particular room. Never knowing sometimes where one might end up in the medical evaluations and processes has sometimes been scary and left me feeling perplexed with chronic anxiety.

Thinking back over all of the challenges and changes in my life and health, I've often wondered, "Whose life am I living anyway?" I have felt totally discombobulated at times regarding my body parts being here and there; finally put back into their rightful places. I can honesty divulge that my faith has indeed been tried and tested many times over between the above written challenges and other encounters which I have alluded to in this book. They have presented a funny way of working themselves into patience as the verse above denotes.

I can't say that I have felt it all joy to be in such predicaments at the time. What I can say is that God has continuously given me favor and exalted me in my times of illness, weaknesses and set-backs on to my recoveries. Had it not been for the Lord on my side, I truly don't know where I would have been without His presence and healing. I know that He sent angels around to cover and protect me in my daily strife and sufferings. And it is here that I find joy in my travail to know that God once again has delivered me fully.

I am able-bodied and fully functioning in my daily life. Alert in body, mind, and spirit in my faith for the Lord. Therefore, I know that God has given me favor in my life and I know that much work still needs to be done by me for His glory here on earth. Words cannot state how much I thank our Heavenly Father for what He has done in my life and allowed me to be a faithful servant of His. Allowing me to write this book is a point of honor in that it affords me the opportunity to praise Him for all that He continues to work in my life.

How often have you felt patient favor while being admitted into the hospital or going forth in a medical or surgical procedure? Did you ask God to give you faith in all that you were about to endure and whatever processes laid before you? Were you able to develop patience from your faith in the healing of your body and all of its infirmities? If not, ask God for His wisdom and healing in your health matters.

Revelation: Thank you, Jesus, for letting me grow in faith right before my eyes.

Endeavor: Might we forever grow into Your anointed favor as patients seeking healing and wellness.

Prayer: Please, Father, give us the serenity to change our spirits and attitudes in our healthcare with You as our head. May we come to know Your difference in our faith and patience to become honorable patients according to Your will. Amen.

PATIENCE MY CHILD

"And let us not be weary in well doing; for in due season we shall reap if we faint not".

GALATIANS 6:9 (NKJV)

I had situations develop on my job which resulted in my suffering from Post-Traumatic Stress Disorder (PTSD) and having to file a Workman's Compensation claim. It lasted almost two years and I was kept from working via my doctor's orders. My husband was retired and was a comfort of solace for me under the tremendous pressure. We thanked and praised God for our ability to function within our means as time continued to drag along for what seemed forever.

At one point, it appeared that the case would be expedited, but as it turned out, the other party took their time. As the judge set a date within another couple of weeks that they would either have to settle or we would most definitely go to trial, I became even more immersed in prayer and Bible study with my husband and church family thinking that that would solve everything.

It did not but remember, I was tired and worn out from worry. I asked God for patience within my being to help calm down my panicky anxiousness and weary spirit that just could not seem to settle down throughout the process. As my depression grew even heavier by the moment, I heard God say, "Patience my child. I've got this and don't ever forget to put Me first in all of your trials and tribulations!"

Following a few days later, God came pouring through to my immediate rescue and saved me from undergoing a trial as a settlement decision finally resulted in my favor. So, how could I give up the fight as I knew not when my deliverance would come? I asked after the fact. I humbly thanked God for my victory and wept some tears. It seemed that I had made it through after all! As long and drawn out that the process seemed to be, I was elated and felt victorious in my fight.

How often do we think that our situation is a losing battle? That we are down for the biggest battle in our lifetime with no troops to back us up? Feeling desolate, lost, set astray or maybe, even targeted, we ponder what may be our circumstances in the moment... let alone, the future? It is not like we asked for our situation to befall us as things can just happen right before our eyes. I thanked God again for the patience which He had exhibited within me, His child. As indeed, I was one hot mess!

Revelation: The Holy Spirit helped me to know that I would overcome all obstacles in due time.

Endeavor: I ask that we remember that our blessing will come in a little while if we but have patience and wait upon God.

Prayer: Help us to cast our cares upon our Heavenly Father at all times as His children. Allow us to derive Your will, Lord, through the Holy Spirit to invoke within us strength, fortitude, and a passion for victory versus a self-defeating attitude. Amen.

SLOWLY BREWING

"And you will seek me and find me, when you search for me with all your heart."

JEREMIAH 29:13 (NKJV)

Literally, I had a coffee pot that took about an hour to brew ten cups of coffee. Obviously, it had become damaged, however I was determined to hold out and just not buy another coffee maker. After all, it was given to me by my daughter and is my favorite color--- red. There was far too much sentimentality going on here not to keep it despite its faulty equipment. And the coffee tasted really good in fact, slowly brewing!

Then again, my husband and I could wait for our cups of coffee watching the short drips of fluid sieving out into the carafe for over a half hour. We could hear its loud moans of utter disgust and anxiety in trying to perform its job, but we became immune and couldn't let go anyway. After all, it had a job to do in its own time and we could wait.

And during all of that down time, it gave my husband and I opportunities to seek God, whether through television evangelists preaching the word or an open discussion of particular scriptures or characters themselves from the Bible. As we read from various versions such as the King James, New King James, Amplified, and so forth, we indeed found God with all of our hearts throughout the pages.

Suddenly on one particular day, I began to think upon other aspects of my life as to my ability to let go of past unforeseen circumstances and other situations that had come to a halt and literally died. Had I failed to let go of them I now asked myself. Upon further reflection, I had. It had all become about control and my need to win over... even if it was a coffee pot's death this time.

Yet, what about our human interactions and relationships? Just how far will we let others lead us in the wrong direction as problems slowly brew and we lean not upon God's promises but our own faulty devices left to brew? Do we seek Him with all of our heart? Or, just give Him tastes of the bitterness left behind? What would be so hard to just let go, and let God into our hearts?

Revelation: Learn to let go and let God into our cracked and worn souls.

Endeavor: Help us to humble ourselves in thoughts and deeds to God's daily will.

Prayer: Remember that God is the head and not the tail of our hearts. Equally in our relationships... be them friendships, marital partners, or relatives that we don't just let our relationships malfunction and die. But that we put a human, loving touch of repair, upkeep, and luster into our relationships given and blessed by the Lord. Amen.

STANDING ON SHAKY GROUND

Whosoever cometh to me, and heareth my sayings, and doeth them, I will shew you to whom he is like. He is like a man who built a house, and digged deep, and laid the foundation on a rock: and when the flood arose, the stream beat vehemently upon that house, and could not shake it: for it was founded upon a rock. But he that heareth, and doeth not, is like a man that without a foundation built a house upon the earth, against which the steam did beat vehemently, and immediately it fell; and the rain of that house was great.

LUKE 6: 47-49

This story is like unto the parable of Jesus from the Sermon on the Mount as well as the Sermon on the Plains. The man who builds his house upon sand results in pure failure as the house cannot withstand the torrential rains having no solid foundational structure and down it falls from standing on shaky ground versus standing on a rock. Which lends the question to men and women concerning their spiritual foundation for life. Is it built upon a solid foundation in Jesus Christ or built upon a cult or other factional group or concept?

Let's look at what Jesus Christ does offer us. Most importantly, our salvation according to John 3:16 and 17. For God so loved the world (man) that He gave His only begotten son Christ Jesus, that whosoever believeth in Him should not perish, but have everlasting life. For God sent not His Son into the world to condemn the world; but that the world through Him might be saved. Without God's promises of everlasting life, where would our lives be… but lost in this world's sins.

Therefore, depending upon whom we choose to follow, study under, and become mentored and led by in our spiritual food and nutritional values, they may ultimately lead to the demise of our very souls. God, working through Jesus Christ and the Holy Spirit (the blessed Trinity), offers us sustenance in our daily diet. Something that we can plan for, buy for, and structure into our very being daily through reading God's Word (the Bible) and writing into journal form… the heart of our every need directed towards our Father which art in Heaven.

Blessed be the Word recorded into our hearts and minds and shaped into our very existence today, tomorrow, and into eternity forever and ever! May we remember to bring others on board along our journeys. And let us learn to be as conductors on the railroad or pilots in the sky helping to navigate the passengers' coastal terrains and wayward skylines toward heaven in all things asking God's guidance as He directs our paths toward solid ground in Christ Jesus.

How many of us see the scenario between building a house or structure on solid ground (rock) versus sand in our Christian faith? Does reading and listening to the Word actually strengthen us in our faith partnership with Christ Jesus? How can what we learn in God's teachings actually prepare us as conductors and pilots in our own lives for others' salvation? May our work on earth then prepare us for our salvation in heaven?

Revelation: May we as Christians continue to conduct and pilot the course for our lost brothers and sisters in uncharted destinies looking for sustenance in Christ Jesus.

Endeavor: Allow us to continue building Your spiritual foundations for Your children here on solid ground.

Prayer: Help us, Lord, to remember Your only begotten Son, Jesus and how He hung on that cross for our sins, thus saving us and giving us eternal life. Help us to remember Jesus as the solid rock upon which our faith was built. Amen.

PEACE

(A State of Freedom from
Turmoil or Quiet)

PEACE BE STILL

"Peace I leave with you, my peace I give to you;
not as the world gives do I give to you.
Let not your heart be troubled, neither let it be afraid."

ST. JOHN 14:27 (NKJV)

The clock had been ticking away and there was no end to the hemorrhaging which was taking place from my mother's left inverted hip. She had suffered a fall at the hospital's emergency room and been hospitalized for several weeks experiencing a failed hip surgery and multiple blood transfusions. All of her life of 44 years she had been hospitalized about every 6-8 weeks, receiving blood transfusions, and being a guinea pig for testing or the next available treatment for her disease at the University hospital. She had given birth to six children despite her illness; three whom lived and three whom died.

Momma had been born with Sickle Cell Anemia, a red blood cell disorder which was chronic, crippling and terminal. She had suffered all of her life in deep pain going in and out of crises. I was the only child present at Momma's death and believed that I saw the death angel appear unto the foot of her bed. Likewise, I believed that I witnessed my mother's separation of her soul from her body as she went home to Jesus in glory. It was all so overwhelming, yet beautiful at the same time.

The whole experience initially frightened me and I had to leave her room. However, the power of the Holy Spirit came and gently quieted my spirit making me no longer troubled and afraid as I felt peace within my soul. I think too, the way my mother embraced her home-going soothed me as well. She appeared as a bright light all shiny and sparkling to my naked eyes bound and ready to go home to glory.

Are you ready to face the death of a loved one and let go? Even when he or she is bound to see the face of God and be embraced in His arms in your daily witness? Have you made peace yourself with our Lord before your demise? How can we become ready? Seek the Lord, read the Bible and speak to your pastor or a clergy. Start working on your homeward and homebound journey immediately getting your salvation in order.

Revelation: Thankfulness for the still inner peace God leaves with us.

Endeavor: Thanks for the peace and courage the Holy Trinity gives us amidst the troubled and fearful waters. Help us to see the rainbows amidst the beautiful and brilliant lights which may surround us during a homegoing.

Prayer: Thank you, Lord, for helping us to keep our minds stayed upon You even in times of confusion, fear, uncertainty, and loss amidst the troubled waters. Enable us to focus upon You and Your goodness and mercy in heaven. Amen.

STRESSFUL REUNIONS

Now I beseech you brethren, by the name of our Lord Jesus Christ, that ye all speak the same thing, and that there be no divisions among you; but that ye be perfectly joined together in the same mind and in the same judgement.

I CORINTHIANS 1:10

Although this is Paul an apostle of Jesus Christ who preached the gospel and talked to the church saints of God at Corinth, he thanks God for His grace given by Jesus Christ. Paul goes on to speak about how God has chosen the foolish things of the world to confound the wise; and God hath chosen the weak things of the world to confound the things which are mighty. That according as it is written, He that glorieth, let him glory in the Lord. I Corinthians 27, 28, 31.

It is obvious that Paul most definitely had the mission and assignment as an apostle. How he tactfully moved from this place to that place and this group of people to that confers to us about his devotion to Jesus Christ. He was shielded and sanctified all along his journeys. Acting as a messenger of God's truth, wisdom, and power, Paul was most honored yet humbled to do God's work amongst the people bringing many of them together in the same mind and same judgement.

Preaching saved those who were unchurched, non-believers who wanted to believe in the Lord. God brought to fruition those things that were not as if they were. Non-intrusively, what was not a reality became as real from God in a matter of moments or seconds unbeknown to the human eye. We are then brought into the sanctity of Christ through His omnipresent wisdom, righteousness and redemption. As it is written, let men glory in Him.

Reunions come in all forms: family, church, school classes, lost friends, Weight Watchers, training partners, military units, misplaced allegiances, businesses or trades, fraternities and sororities, dog shows, reality television shows, and game shows to name a few. However, our goals being unity, conformity, resolve, and tranquility in our working and loving relationships with one another no matter the venue. God says we must adhere and cause no division amongst us.

We should remember the work of Paul and become modern-day apostles of Christ in our relationships and interactions. Let us take the lead in our social circles and with loved ones to help those needing guidance and support from our Father making Him the head and not the tail. May we continue to be a beacon of hope to those who feel unhinged in mind, body, and soul who choose not to work in solidarity.

When was the last time that you gathered together with your loved ones whether family, friends, or otherwise and experienced stress-free versus stressful reunions whether at home, church or another venue? Quite simply, what would you prefer the outcome to be; unity or division, hatred or love, productivity or malaise in working together on the same accord? Let us be about the tasks of becoming blessed peacemakers as spoken by Jesus in the Beatitudes.

Revelation: Working together on the same accord, we can make a difference in the Lord.

Endeavor: Allow all people to become magnified on earth as we glory in the Lord absent of stressful reunions amongst ourselves.

Prayer: Help us to work as Paul in bringing together God's flock of peacemakers. Possibly, one can take the lead to work out the soul-salvation of the particular group in question. So rather than creating an atmosphere of disarray and mutiny… therein will rest in harmony and peace for all involved. Amen.

HALLELUJAH, MY FATHER

*Train up a child in the way he should go: and
when he is old, he will not depart from it.*

PROVERBS 22:6

Life between our father and my brother wasn't always an easy or a clear pathway. As a matter of fact, I am sure that it was a pretty common relationship seen between a father and his son today. Not unlike the Lord and His son, Jesus as most sons try to emulate their fathers in words, thoughts, and deeds as their dearest and nearest role models in their daily lives.

Certainly, my brother's life differed in many ways from our father, but our father was the head, guide, instructor, and living testament "hands on guy" that led the way for my brother. I will refer to words previously written in "Not My Will, Lord" below as was lived and witnessed by our earthly father, James, to use in this entry as well.

James was a man of simple but earnest means who went to work every day trying to secure a livelihood for his family and minimal property... house and car. He and his brother had lost their mother to death early in life as teenagers as she died at age 32. They were left to the hands of a cruel stepfather who often abused them so they learned how to street fight and box to take care of themselves. Eventually, he dropped out of school in ninth grade but had a dream of entering the military, specifically the Army.

Instead, Daddy married very young at seventeen and he and my mother gave birth to six babies, losing three in death. He grew bitter at times with all the responsibility that was on him as our mother was sickly and suffered tremendously from a blood disorder but he took care of her and us as best as he could. He did have other vices which got him into trouble in his life and stirred the pot in our parents' marriage which I recall.

They stayed together anyway rearing three adolescents to adulthood and marriage. Two of the three children enrolled in the Air Force and our sister became a Captain with advanced degrees and my brother earned his Bachelor's, then became an executive within a food distribution company. All three children earned college degrees. I became a classroom teacher and health educator employed through several school districts and the local health department.

All three of us are retired today from our respective positions. But my brother is the one in which I want to highlight as he observed and watched my father from the perspective of a mentor and example of what fatherhood should be like. Daddy taught him so much from what he did accomplish due to his level of education, opportunities, and family supports. My brother has indeed been a faithful student and son as outlined by God according to the Bible.

Train up a child in the way he should go and when he is old, he will not depart from it. That is what my twin did along his life's journey and it placed him in a very stable, affluent, and beneficial place in society as we know it today. This is not to say that we girls did not have the same opportunities and blessings because we did. I just want to highlight my brother as being an African-American male and the spiritual peace which he achieved in his life despite societal and cultural statistics due to his choice decisions.

Daddy instilled in him a work ethic which has carried with him throughout his career. From delivering newspapers, to working at fast food chains to door to door selling. While doors were closed to our father, my brother took advantage of opportunities such as educational benefits through the GI Bill after serving in the U.S. Air Force.

While in college he became interested in the financial markets where he took an interest in stocks. Gains in this area afforded him the opportunity to assist the family financially when it was needed throughout the years. And I believe that this is an area which is a gift of my brother's given by the Lord.

My brother has been married to his wife for over twenty-five years and has one daughter. He and his family know what it means to give service to others and serve the Lord. Just how important is it to understand our familial past and where we came from in order to move forward in our lives and help others? Obviously, God instilled much from His Heavenly Father unto his son, James to pass on.

Does God use both willing and unwilling individuals to work His plans here on earth and spread His goodwill? To what degree do we give God the glory for our trials and tribulations as well as successes experienced in life's lessons? Can we find the resolution of peace which only God can give within ourselves to then share amongst others for the better good? Can we cry, "Hallelujah, My Father, for what He has done in our lives?"

Revelation: "Hallelujah, My Father," should be stated by all Christians in thanks and praise to our fathers here on earth!

Endeavor: May we forever give reverence to our fathers for the teaching seen and unseen for which we gleaned and learned from, thus proceeding and succeeding in the Lord's teachings as we grew up and grew older in life to eventually pass on to our own seeds in Christ Jesus.

Prayer: Help us, Lord, to remember our upbringings arising from our families, in particular our fathers as head of household with no disrespect toward the mother of the home who might be the head. Amen

LIGHT OF THE MOON

That He would grant unto us, that we, being delivered out of the hand of our enemies, might serve Him without fear. To give light to them that sit in darkness and in the shadow of death, to guide our feet into the way of peace.

LUKE 1:74; 79

There are various sections in the Bible which refer to scripture that implies happenings occurring during the darkened hours of the evening or late night into early morning while traveling under the light of the moon. Of course, this often happened to protect the parties involved from being seen or revealed possibly to their enemies or in the case of war and surprise attacks. The goal would be to become delivered out of the hand of the enemies and serve God without fear while sitting or walking in darkness and in the shadow of death.

Or such travel took place by the light of the moon because one did not want to travel under the heat of a hot day. Then again, depending upon one's destiny, it could have all come down to timing and wanting to rest or be in a place by early morning to carry out one's business. Some others might have figured that road volume would have been less busy during the night so travel then. Or, better yet…if one's not tired from traveling all day and wants to continue during the night, continue forth anyway to your chosen location.

Still, others may have reckoned that they found peace traveling under the moon and stars with just enough light to lead them on to their destinations. Just to name a few occurrences whereby men and women travelled by the light of the moon in the Bible I will note as follows: when Joseph and Mary fled to Egypt after giving birth to Jesus fleeing from King Herod and his men as stated by the angel of the Lord. Or, the three friends who followed the Star of the East traveling to find Job in his desolation.

Then there was Rahab, the harlot who protected her household from the soldiers who were searching for Joshua and Caleb who were spying out the land, but let them flee quietly during the night. Gideon was able to route the Midianites to a place away from his men. And Nicodemus came to Jesus (Rabbi) at night and asked the Lord how he might be saved and enter the Kingdom of Heaven. Or when Job himself shaved his head and threw ashes from the firepit over his head and body mourning all of the losses which he had endured in his grieving from the days throughout the nights.

Giving light to those which sit in darkness and in the shadow of death, guiding one's path to peace we have to remember those suffering from mental health disorders today such as clinical depression, anxiety, bipolar, and schizophrenia. Or sit in seclusion and isolation living with the Covid virus or its variants, heart and lung or other diseases and disorders. Hopefully, most will be delivered and freed from whatever aversion or ailment they are suffering from and come into total peace with our Lord if they let go and let God work His wonderful miracle of healing if it be His will.

Through it all, we must give God the glory to then allow ourselves His peace which comes from our understanding of His destination for our footpaths. We must recognize and know God's peace that rests with us in our moments of darkness and disease. That even though we suffer, so shall we find peace if we let God enter in. It has to be a conscious decision made under the light of the moon if that is where we are at spiritually, else He will not enter into our hearts and minds.

Many folks have been left hanging on the edge because they felt they had no other alternative to their illness or situation at hand. I am sure that most of the people whom I wrote about earlier who travelled under the light of the moon came to know of the God whom they served and found gave them peace in their travels along their journeys. Let us learn to let Jesus be a light unto our paths in our daily walk with Him.

How many of us cringe or stumble in the middle of the night going to the bathroom or into the kitchen to get something to eat or drink? Can we say that we know our way around our surroundings well enough that we just walk there otherwise? Or do we say that we cannot find our way unless a light is on and set for us viewing our pathway? The point being, if we have built a peaceable relationship with the Lord on either a dark walkway or a lighted pathway, He will be there to receive us with open arms under the light of the moon or the sunshine at the end of the rainbow.

Revelation: We know that God can provide peace no matter our circumstances.

Endeavor: Lord, we ask that we find Your goodness, grace, mercy, and forgiveness even under the light of the moon.

Prayer: May we hold on to God's promises in learning what His destination is for our lives. And I believe that means moving from a place of darkness to lightness. Blessed be the Lord who continues to lead and guide us by His words. And when we are lost, will lead us home once again. Amen.

WATER DANCES

Whispering raindrops lightly abound…
gently pounding their glistening droplets
as newborn babies covered in vernix
and sucking their thumbs in synchronization.

Emerging head-first, most glide slowly…
others move rapidly, while some become stuck
before ejecting themselves freely from the
parachutes of their mother's wombs.

Landing safely with the help of their
tightly woven umbilical cords…
crying lightly, possibly screaming loudly or
a few squirming quietly upon their descent.

Several might be making ugly faces…
while others, simply smile quite happily
along their sea-faring voyages down
through the panoramic canals.

Pulsating sounds of water wildly beat…
rapidly growing into gusting winds
formed like funnel clouds as cotton
candy on long, cylindrical drumsticks.

Prancing, then galloping while making
quivering sounds as horses… nudging their
noses and caressing their bodies as the waters
run across the rivers and lakes into their parents' arms.

Rhythmically, they shake and resound loudly as
musical instruments colliding into crescendos…
magically stepping to the Tango, Ballet, Tap,
Bump, Twister, Hip Hop and Electric Slide.

Exhaustingly dancing together, they electrify
each other from morning until night…
positively charging and challenging each other's
dance steps until they dance no longer and sleep.

Written by Donna Collier Rickman

PERSEVERANCE

(Persists in an undertaking despite
opposition or discouragement)

CALCULATING MY NET WORTH

But we all, with open face beholding as in a glass the glory of the Lord, are changed into the same image from glory to glory, even as by the Spirit of the Lord.

II CORINTHIANS 3:18

As a young girl between the ages of five to about eight, my hair had undergone rigorous changes and it had become not what my mother wanted it to be. Longer and manageable with a comb or brush and not under siege in order to perform like the so-called good Negro girl's hair did. Comb simply and be braided and taken down again with ease quite routinely. No hot comb necessarily applied for straightening. Just natural locks.

Instead, my mother underwent a rigorous program to encourage mostly natural growth, luster, and fullness whereby, after washing it she would separate it into corn-rolled braids and finger-place Sulfur 8 hair grease throughout the rows and deep down into the crevices of each hair follicle. Following, I had to wear a cut-off stocking cap up to its thigh area on my hair in public at grade school… all the way through to fourth grade many times.

I think that between the white students and teachers, along with a few of us Negro kids… they just got used to the practice and the smell. Again, such steps were taken to embolden my unacceptable grade of hair and encourage a natural growth process instead. Also, when Momma would take it down, it would be more ready to then be straightened out with the ever-heated straightening comb she'd prepared in my waiting.

Weeks seemed to go past into months and then years as this process proceeded. Later, there appeared to be some progress as my hair did thicken and seemed to become more manageable. It grew longer than Momma's fingertips allowing her some locks to hold onto and press. But, boy, the moisture that generated from that heat after my hair had been washed was most unforgettable. I felt most definitely ashamed of myself.

I cried each and every time and felt total disdain in such practices as I screamed and hollered for dear life. I always prayed that I had good hair and could wear long flowing locks going down my back. Why, I even wished for the flow and length of white girl's hair instead. As I would be allowed to place my hands into a friend's hair whenever I so chose, a Negro teacher I had, absolutely abhorred it and let me readily know it. I did it anyway because I dreamed of better hair days for myself.

Throughout Junior High and High school, I wore a natural Afro which did grow and fill in well. I was proud of it. Possibly, the Sulfur 8 did make an alarming unknown difference doing its silent work as promised. The Afro became my namesake hair-do until the Jheri Curl and I wore it that way into my mid-thirties. Soon after, I ventured into some other hairstyles that were current at the time.

I decided to try some hair tracks. They were generally glued in and yes, I had heard about possible hair loss from the glue but I just loved the way that straight hair could be added onto my own at varying lengths, colors, and styles remembering that is what I had wanted since grade school. In time, I started suffering from some bald areas from hair loss, however I then decided to get extra tracks further glued in. After all, they weren't permanent.

Soon, I was going to the beauty salons for braids, long and short, crochets and other hair sew-ins, and wig sew-ins over time because I had no choice. I had literally begun to lose even more small clumps of hair, presumably from various usages of glue and other hair products over the years. Even braiding added extra weight, thus pull to the scalp which I thought may have contributed to hair loss as well.

I really didn't know what to think. Possibly, I had made some really bad choices in my hair regiments and was now paying the price in later life. My beautician of over ten years began to think differently…

that maybe it was not all due to hair glue usage through the years and changes which affected my own hair growth.

Sometime after, I noticed hair loss over most of my body and more balding spots in my scalp. Both my beautician and myself began to look at the whole situation differently concluding that I was instead dealing with real hair loss now, called alopecia. And having had an autoimmune disorder did not help matters either.

It had taken me some time to accept such a condition as it changed my body, mindset, image, and definitely made me find other ways to wear and style the hair pieces, weaves, or wigs for whatever styles I had chosen to wear. At least I had a choice in the matter I concluded.

My mother was quite the Christian to see beyond the human face or perceived image which I had of myself and looked unto the Lord for reassurance and perseverance. She helped me in many ways to try and accept in the mirror what God had given to me as my own crown of glory...even though I could not see it.

I guess that it's really not a big deal any more in today's era as most movie stars and singers do the same thing in their everyday lives without any questions or problems. But instead, make hair a beauty statement. Just the same, at times. I miss the days of my Afro or Jheri Curl minus the greasy hairspray and the full, lustrous, and natural locks that I displayed throughout my head.

My hair really became an investment in my calculating my own net or self-worth in society during those years. Throughout all of the changes and fallacies in some cases regarding my own, vain justifications, the Lord allowed me to reflect differently about my reality and put me in check so to speak about what the importance of such an item really was about.

Quite simply, it does not necessarily make me a more even-keeled, loving and beautiful person on the inside. But it is what is in the inside which the Lord has bestowed within me with natural grace and beauty that counts on the outside. I thank my Heavenly Father for all of the times that I had gone through in childhood to get a full head of hair.

And to that, I give thanks to my mother for that was all that she knew in trying to make my hair manageable and to help me to cope. Do or can we as children see to put the pieces together being placed before our eyes? Is it enough to listen to our mother and try to comprehend her teachings? Or rather do we discount her experience, wisdom, and love for doom instead? Most importantly, do we hear her teachings as set forth from the Bible and persevere in our quest?

Revelation: We need to come to realize that in calculating our own net worth, it lies with and in the Lord above, not earthly visions.

Endeavor: Help us to persevere and look beyond the mirror of self-humiliation and shame unto the grace of our Heavenly Father.

Prayer: We sincerely need prayer to forever honor and trust the words, assurances, and guidance of our mothers through the years. And as we grow into adulthood, worth, and wisdom... may we remember the God-given teachings of our mothers who were forever our best buddies looking out for our well-being. Amen.

COUNTING THE MOMENTS

The righteous cry, and the Lord heareth, and delivereth
them out of all their troubles. Many are the afflictions of
the righteous: but the Lord delivereth him out of them all.

PSALM 15:17,19

For years, I had struggled with hernias located throughout my body here and there. Origins resulted from heavy lifting to just plain moving the wrong way. One had come through the inguinal canal resting in an awkward position, another in the posterior, and yet another in the anterior of my intestine. Finally, I had reached a point whereby, I was looking six-seven months pregnant and not having any form of elimination.

After being admitted and sent into my hospital room one afternoon, upon eating lunch I soon found out another problem presented itself from my intestinal tract. And that was that I was experiencing an Ileus, a complete bowel obstruction. I had begun vomiting profusely and had been unable for days to produce any waste material.

Within moments, nurses had planted an NG (nasal gastrointestinal) tube down my nose and into my stomach. The purpose, to collect any and all fluids before going into my gastric intestinal tract to be filtered out into a jar. It was absolutely revolting to see that waste. It seemed that without this procedure, I would have continually kept vomiting because of food in my stomach not being digested on through my intestinal tract.

I was due for surgery to determine the cause of the Ileus. I had it but nothing resolved itself for six days. There was still absolutely no movement of my bowels. My abdomen continued extending. Cat scans were still showing no movement. The surgeon determined in my second week of hospitalization, that he needed to go back in surgically and examine my intestinal tract again… seeing if there was something that had been overlooked.

In the meantime, my abdomen was expanding and now becoming darker in color. Cat scans were continuously being taken on a daily basis in hopes of finding some resolution to my problem; some sign of movement, even flatulence of any amount.

I was growing more anxious by each day as I began counting the moments in and of themselves. I remember crying out to the Lord and praying that there were not any signs of gangrene going on from lack of blood circulation. I screamed at the surgeon and demanded answers concerning my overall health, let alone from what was going on inside of me which appeared to be nothing.

Days on end, I tried even forcing myself to create some kind of movement beyond the secretions from out of my stomach throughout the tube and into the jar. With all of the fluid and waste that were discharging themselves, it scared me as I knew I hadn't eaten or taken in any foods orally for weeks.

The surgeon almost seemed scared himself talking about Ileuses were the "bane to his existence" and that many of his patients were for some reason getting them. Frankly, that concerned me because I knew that I still had an Ileus going on and my abdomen was still extending itself. I looked like I was about to deliver in childbirth and my abdomen was even darker. The thought of gangrene still frightened me terribly as I would cry out in frustration, lost hope, and terror to God.

Again, the surgeon tried to assure me that things internally were fine but I felt him questioning my situation as well. The next day, he came in and announced that I would be having my third surgery in three weeks to determine exactly what had been and was going on inside my intestinal tract. I recall him drawing a diagram on a white board and he and a nurse trying to explain to me what they hoped to do the next day surgically. All I know is that I needed relief as soon as possible.

It seemed that each time the surgeon went in, he physically untwisted my intestines inspecting each and every dimension of them to find the cause for the Ileus. Hopefully, the third time would be the charm and give him the answers we were all hoping for. Also, whether my Ileus was resulting from a physical or mechanical blockage was yet to be determined and I might need sections of bowel removed (which I had previously undergone in hernia surgeries when mesh got caught up).

Now that I was out of recovery and into my room, I could hear the nurses rejoicing that the problem had been resolved. Finally, no more surgeries and I had movement from all ends and throughout my intestines. So, after three weeks of surgery and almost 21 days of hospitalization, I would at last be able to go home.

You can't imagine the genuine joy and relief I felt from hearing such news! They actually hadn't been hernia surgeries but they were associated with the problems I was undergoing with the Ileus. I thanked the Holy Trinity: Father, Son and Holy Ghost for my deliverance and healing to come through these afflictions in my body. Surely, God had listened and heard my cries, uncertainties, and dilemmas, thus brought me out of them and made me whole again.

How many of you have been delivered and healed from certain afflictions knowing that God had your backs? Are you witnessing to others about the greatness of God having heard your pleas? If you met God the next day and went home to glory, rather than recovery on earth, would you still glorify God's omnipotence in your life?

Revelation: Life and death can be too close to call sometimes so we must remember our Maker daily before all of our trials.

Endeavor: To get our minds and bodies stayed on the Lord for we don't know the time or day we might go home in glory.

Prayer: Remind us, Lord, that You are the healer and deliverer out of our greatest afflictions. Without You, we can become so lost and displaced in our Christianity and reverence for our Maker's promises of total healing in our bodies, minds, and spirits. Amen.

KNOCKING DOWN A BRICKHOUSE

But now thus saith the Lord that created thee, O Jacob and He that formed thee, O Israel, Fear not: for I have redeemed thee, I have called thee by name; thou art mine. When thou passest through the waters, I will be with thee: and through the rivers, they shall not overflow thee: when thou walkest through the fire, thou shalt not be burned, neither shall the flame kindle upon thee.

ISAIAH 43:1-2

Remember the story of the three little pigs… I will paraphrase a line of text intertwined within my own words to sum up the story as I recall it for my readers. Help us to revisit the story as follows. "I am going to huff and puff and blow your house down" through straw, sticks, and bricks. Just watch and see what I the big, bad wolf can and shall do my little fella pigs. Hah, hah, hah! The wolf blows through two structures losing to one of them…the brickhouse as he perseveres.

The story talks about structures. Houses which were built with different substances and how they were knocked down by the blow of air while the brickhouse withstood all of the wolf's blows. Of course, it is a children's story but it adds depths of truth to the power of the story and reality of God's word. Why? Because of its composition or make-up versus those of the straw and sticks. I mean visually, I would like everyone to think about the thickness and solidity of the bricks over the straw and sticks in real time. Simply, what do we already know?

Absolutely, no comparison in likeness in mass, density or poundage. Correct? It's the same with Jesus Christ. In Him, nothing else can ever compare. We can live and die remembering how God sacrificed His Son's life for all of ours. Therefore, who else or what else can we even think about serving that would be equal to our Father in Heaven who cannot be knocked down…ever! And, certainly Lucifer himself cannot supply us with everlasting life as our brickhouse to salvation. But he can be knocked down or knocked out through the power of the Holy Trinity and prayer.

We must remember that the Lord created us and formed our world in which we live. He also knows us by name and all of the hairs upon our heads. When we walk with Him, we never walk alone. He is forever there shielding and guarding our every being through waters and fire or whatever obstacle we might encounter as we persevere just as the Israelites did. Obstacles or brick houses that can overtake us include lack of finances and housing, drugs, alcohol, gambling, physical and mental abuses, acts of war, climate and weather changes and the like.

God gives us His Son to trust in and cling to in helping us out in such times to overcome such brick houses and knock them down forever out of our lives. But if such powers should actually overpower us as human beings in real time, God just releases our human bodies and brings our souls home to glory with Him. He never lets go or leaves us alone which is what we must come to know and remember no matter the circumstance and outcome. Equally, we must surrender ourselves to God as well in our challenges on earth so that He can renew and restore our salvation in Him.

How many brick houses do we have that need to be knocked down in our lives to serve our Lord and Savior righteously? Can we reason in ourselves that such a brick house can withstand the elements or need to be knocked down on our road to salvation with our Father? Do we need to huff and puff to view the results or do we already know the substance of our essence in Christ Jesus? If we lose sight, can we make a comeback and withstand the blows to our brick house of salvation?

Revelation: We know that we can do all things through Christ Jesus if we just persevere in Him.

Endeavor: May we all learn how to check into our salvation with the Lord through assessing our daily walk with and in Him.

Prayer: Help us, Lord, to check our substance or essence covered in You. For when we walketh through the waters or river and get caught in the fire or flames, they shall not overtake us for You shall be there as our rock never to be knocked down by any brick house in our road. Amen.

WHAT SAYS THIS MAN?

And it came to pass, when Jesus had made an end of commanding His twelve disciples, He departed thence to teach and to preach in their cities. Now when John had heard in the prison the words of Christ, he sent two of his disciples. And said unto Him, Art thou He that should come, or do we look for another? Jesus answered and said unto them, Go and shew John again those things which ye do hear and see: The blind receive their sight, and the lame walk, the lepers are cleansed, and the deaf hear, the dead are raised up, and the poor have the gospel preached to them. And blessed is he, whosoever shall not be offended in me.

MATTHEW 11:1-6

What says this man? Obviously, there came a day when Jesus had to declare through His perseverance that His mentorship with His twelve disciples had been completed and come to an end, thus time for Him to move on. It would be left for them to follow the examples of Jesus Christ in their healings, teachings, and preaching of the Lord for the benefit of the peoples whom the disciples would encounter in their journeys across the lands. And as usual, Jesus left to follow suit with His teachings and preaching in the cities where the disciples lived. Keep in mind that Jesus had been crucified, dead, and buried before raising up on the third day and walking and talking amongst the people as a shining example of the power of the Lord (our most Holy and merciful Father).

Sadly enough, not everyone who encountered Jesus thought or believed Him to be the great Messiah and Deliverer of God's Truth, with healings to bestow and Christ's teachings to be taught. Simply, they were naysayers. With that being said, John had heard of the teachings of the great Messiah while in prison but did not necessarily believe that the words were from Him. Jesus' rebuttal to John's disciples were to show John what they had witnessed in their everyday encounters themselves amongst the masses of people looking at the blind who now see, the lame who now walk, the lepers who are healed, the dead whom are brought back to life, and the poor who were preached to and received God's words.

And what do you readers suppose our tasks are from the above statements? If you thought or stated to go forth as disciples of Christ ourselves in ministering the good news amongst the people telling of God's works and miracles on earth, I would say that you are partially correct. The other component would be to become as lights within the world showcasing your Christianity for the world to witness in your daily lives. So, not just do God's will, but live it and ask what sayeth the man, Christ Jesus! Therefore, volunteer one's time, talents, and spiritual gifts beyond the doors of the church and branch out working in one's communities, townships, and neighborhoods spreading the good news of our Lord. Let our actions speak to the world as did Jesus.

How do you think that you would have responded if you had been John sitting in prison? And if you are sitting in prison today, what say you about this man named Jesus? How many of you readers believe that you are modern-day disciples for our Lord as you persevere in teaching, preaching, and helping to heal those who are less fortunate within our communities?

How many of you saints believe that you can bring others (deliver) them to Christ today in your service to the Lord? How would one determine their work to be legitimate and not done in vain? Remember what Jesus said regarding your answers: your witness to people's vision restored, ability to walk, bodies healed, ability to hear, the dead brought back to life, the poor hearing the gospel, not witnessing others becoming offended in Christ.

Revelation: Learning that we all can be hearers and doers of the words of Christ Jesus, thus says the Lord.

Endeavor: To remember to look and witness God's presence all around us to legitimize His spirit and presence in our lives.

Prayer: Help us, Lord, to better learn how to become disciples of Your truth for the work on earth to be done according to You. Invoke within us the spirit of learning and teaching by attending Bible study, reading the Bible for own growth and education and being a sunbeam for You. Amen.

REASSURANCE

(Restoring Confidence, Not
Worry or Uncertainty)

BOUNDLESS MERCIES

*"Let not mercy and truth forsake thee; bind them about
your neck, write them upon the table of thine heart."*

PROV. 3:3

About twelve years ago, my husband and I had driven to a town about
forty-five miles from where we lived in hopes of visiting a favorite
restaurant which had much ambience and meaning in our lives.
Throughout the short drive, we reveled in thinking about the food
menu and savoring the wine choices for the day and couldn't wait to
get there.

Rain was pouring down and in order to get to the restaurant, we
had to walk with an umbrella where much construction to buildings was
taking place. We remember just seeing this woman all dressed in a white
garment including a sheet which covered her completely from head to
toe. I honestly do not remember seeing her shoes. She was sitting on
a bench on one side of the street when we entered the courtyard and
thought, "Bless her heart, out here in all of this rain!"

However, upon leaving the restaurant almost two and one-half
hours later we found her still sitting on the bench only now, on a
different side of the street. But who had moved the bench? She couldn't
have done it alone as it was far too heavy! It had literally been moved
from the interior side of the courtyard to the other exterior side some
thirty feet away. We quickly gave her money and blessed it as she spoke
thankfulness to us for it. Yet, we felt perplexed about our role in how
all this was to play out and asked God for reassurance in this matter.

The most which we seemed to garner at that point on our wedding anniversary was our location and the plans which we had to celebrate at one of our favorite restaurants and the nuance which it offered us. Certainly, finding this stranger in our pathway seemed somewhat awkward and removed from real time. Exactly, what was our mission to be played out in this unlikely encounter? Such an encounter where our Christianity was being challenged epically at those moments.

Looking up to the high heavens, we recognized God's presence and felt that our hearts had been touched by an angel of light. Why us and why else was our attention drawn to her? Were others ever receptive to her unlikely presence? If so, we had not recognized their presence. Had God wanted to see if we still had boundless mercies in our hearts as we looked at the truth while witnessing homelessness in the face? We prayed that we did as we "bound them around our neck and wrote them upon the tablet of our hearts."

Revelation: May we forever help those in need wherever we may travel.

Endeavor: Lead us to higher heights in you oh Lord, we do pray looking beyond what we see and witness to a position of serenity in You.

Prayer: Dear Heavenly Father, keep Your omnipotent mercy and truth available in our daily lives. That we might reach out and grasp reality for what it holds for our spirituality today and tomorrow in helping others. Amen.

ELEVATED PRESSURES

"Give, and it shall be given unto you; good measure, pressed down, and shaken together, and running over, shall men give into your bosom. For with the same measure that ye mete, withal it shall be measured to you again."

LUKE 6:38

There are times that we all just have to sit back, breathe and try to absorb all that is going on around us. Momentarily, reality might seem so far off from what we are living in our current, daily lives whether in the workplace, our homes, neighborhoods, communities, and states... let alone, world affairs. We may even be grieving wondering about yesterday and how things used to function and/or exist in the world we once knew and welcomed as home.

It can be all too consuming and overwhelming or delightfully magic and fanciful. But through it all God is forever present and comforting through our good, jubilant, and profitable gains as well as our troubling, exhaustive, and non-productive losses. Through it all, we must be willing to admit our weaknesses, frailties and shortcomings in life to then move on to use our strengths, gifts and talents for God's glory.

There is a season for everything and when God opens up the barnyards, let us humble ourselves and become amenable to His service. Let us be stewards of His word sharing His gifts and talents embodied within us for others. Let us be willing to be good shepherds finding Christ in His flock throughout the world. And let us especially be willing to listen and reach out to others helping them even through our pocketbooks and wallets. For as the verse reminds us, God will do the rest as our elevated pressures will be "Pressed down, shaken together and running over" in our hearts and minds!

Are we ready to let go and let God do His work in our lives today as obedient servants of His? Do we believe that only we can singularly change the world with no hint of help from God? Are we really looking for our purposes here on earth as directed from God? Can we be willing to give more than our wallets and pocketbooks can hold to be used for the glory of God's Kingdom here on earth?

Revelation: The measure which we use will also be measured back to us in our giving.

Endeavor: We must be willing to answer God's call whenever and however it comes.

Prayer: No matter what the circumstances or elevated pressures in our lives, we need to give all that we are able in God's name spiritually, physically, mentally, and monetarily in good measure, pressed down, shaken together, and running over. Amen.

TOUCHED BY AN ANGEL

But we see Jesus, who was made a little lower than the angels for the suffering of death, crowned with glory and honor; that He by the grace of God should taste death for every man. For it became Him, for whom all things, in bringing many sons unto glory, to make the captain of their salvation perfect through sufferings.

HEBREWS 2:9-10

Ever since a young child around nine years old into adulthood, I had been told by my late mother of the power which I had received and still have today in the strength of my hands or touch. She would call upon me each and every time to just rub her body down when she experienced excruciating pain and suffering from her inherited blood disease of Sickle Cell Anemia.

This disease made her bones, muscles, and joints ache horribly to the point of becoming crippling for her in her daily life. It seemed that my rubbing of her body calmed her and gave her peace as she told me, from my gift of healing hands from the Lord. I took her words at heart and began using them as was seen fit accordingly whether as heard from the Lord or felt from deep within my own spirit.

Now, I had been raised up in the church along with my two siblings and we knew of stories from the Bible of Jesus and His disciples and their ability to touch and heal the sick. It was during these times that I had felt a power greater than myself and would just become obedient, focused and guided inspirationally to touch the wounded or affected area(s) of certain individuals who were pointed out to me believing that they would become healed.

There were times that I witnessed individuals needing prayer and a Holy touch which I believed needed to come from the Lord. I was just the instrument of peace at the time. In particular, I was in a retail store one day and saw this young woman struggling with her pregnancy. She was of a smaller frame and I believed that the baby was going to be quite large for her to deliver. She was frantically rubbing her belly as the baby was pushing and jumping around inside of her. I could see this movement from the outside of her clothing to know that she was highly distressed at the time.

Frankly, I wasn't sure if she was in labor or not. Suddenly, I heard a voice tell me to aid her and place my hands upon her stomach in such a way as to quiet the baby. I was not afraid to approach her. At first, I wasn't sure if we could get through a language barrier when I was asking her if I could touch her stomach. However, God intervened and solved all of that. Looking at her face and body movements, I could discern that she was not afraid of me or of what I intended to do to her abdomen.

After allowing me to place both of my hands on her protruding stomach, immediately a change came over her face and the baby quit kicking and jumping around inside of her as before. While I was praying and blessing them, she told me she felt calmer inside… peaceful and then thanked me for helping her out. She sat down for several moments, then got up and went about her business shopping. I thanked God for my gift but the rest was left up to God to do.

Through it all, it has been Jesus Who has suffered for our sins and transgressions and was crowned with glory and honor. He was made a little lower than the angels as He suffered in death for humankind. But had it not been for Christ, then the rest of us could not have followed Him unto glory and been redeemed of our own sufferings through Him.

Are there times when you believe that you have been touched or visited by angels? Have you ever been open and readily available to perform the task(s) set before you? Do you listen for the voice of Christ to direct your actions? You will become a witness to God's presence and His power as that still sweet spirit of peace and goodwill prevails over your actions.

Revelation: Become a willing servant of change and peace for the Lord.

Endeavor: Give us the courage to do Your will as needed in the world to change the hearts of man and woman.

Prayer: Help us not to be afraid to discern the message of the messenger and then, deliver the will and the works of God as He speaks to us. May our sufferings in this lifetime be made lighter through the work of the Holy Spirit Who intercedes on the Lord's behalf toward healing, whole-ness, and salvation as Jesus died for our sins. Amen.

THE BEST OF TIMES

And seeing the multitudes, He went up into a mountain: and when He was set, His disciples came unto Him: And He opened His mouth, and taught them saying, Blessed are the poor in spirit: for theirs's is the kingdom of heaven. Blessed are they that mourn: for they shall be comforted. Blessed are the meek: for they shall inherit the earth. Blessed are they which do hunger and thirst after righteousness: for they shall be filled. Blessed are the merciful: for they shall obtain mercy. Blessed are the pure in heart: for they shall see God. Blessed are the peacemakers: for they shall be called the children of God. Blessed are they which are persecuted for righteousness' sake: for theirs is the kingdom of heaven. Blessed are ye, when men shall revile you, and persecute you, and shall say all manner of evil against you falsely, for my sake.

MATTHEW 5:1-11

Jesus had been talking with four of His disciples, Peter and Andrew who had been fishing by the sea of Galilee and James and John on a ship with their father mending their nets in order to fish. His goal, to make them fishers of men, not just fishermen. He later travelled to the Mount of Olives where He gave His final instructions (sermon on the Beatitudes) to His disciples before ascending into heaven.

What exactly was Jesus talking about and to whom was He targeting in His mission? He was talking about people who had diseases and were being tormented; those who were possessed by devils or were lunatics who had palsy in which He healed them. It seems to me that Jesus gave great care in reassuring those sick with both physical and mental diseases and disorders that the best of times for them were yet to come.

They just had to abide in His will and presence seeking ye the kingdom of heaven and all other good things would be assured to them. With the help of His disciples, they were able to guide and direct the multitudes of followers their way to hear words from Jesus which would be reassuring to their hearts, minds, and souls in seeking some sort of relief from or dealing with their aliments and calamities found in their surroundings.

As written above in the scriptures, Jesus reached His hands inside of the body of people and literally, pulled them out one from another healing them far beyond recognitions making the crooked straight, the weakened strong, the lunatics of sound mind, those with the palsy upright and not bent in any shape or form any longer, and the possessed free of bondage from the devils. Imagine being amongst the massive crowds witnessing the awesomeness of Christ Jesus.

Such multitudes would find the kingdom of heaven here on earth and would come to feel comforted and soothed based on the promises of Jesus that they shall inherit the earth, no longer feel hunger and thirst but become satisfied also in spirit, obtaining mercy, allowing the pure in heart to see God amongst themselves, become peacemakers called the children of God, become persecuted for righteousness' sake, and find blessings amongst all whom have evil words spoken against them for Jesus' sake.

The overwhelming reassurances of healing and peace which Jesus and His disciples poured out providing and backing up their words by their actions must have meant performing miracle after miracle amongst the multitudes that followed them. One cannot even begin to see the wonders which surrounded the crowds that day. Those must have been hallelujah moments giving honor to God our Father in heaven and unto Jesus Christ and His disciples in a job done well above their expectations as they jumped for joy.

It is almost like envisioning families on television in Third World nations obtaining the spiritual word from the ministers and receiving the physical healthcare needs from the doctors in their healing of cleft palates, convocated limbs, famine bodies and ministering of needed mental health treatments and medications. Imagine the blessings which abounded from people's mouths and the release of pressure from their bodies. Blessings pouring out relief from the storms of bad and deadly tides affecting and effecting their daily health which many were simply oblivious to?

Can you imagine having been Jesus before His ascension into heaven? Knowing all that had been accomplished in His work on earth with the following of His disciples and to have to leave it? To have been witness to all of the miracles in that day must have been epic, without fail to the eyes which saw. In light of Covid and all of the deadly ailments and side effects it has caused in nations today, how many of us believe that God can bring it to an end with the help of the CDC and NIH vaccinations? Do we believe that the vaccinations were given to us by God to heal our bodies like in the days of polio, measles and mumps, and the like?

Revelation: May we all look back and read the Beatitudes for consolation to our bodies, minds, and spirits as the best of times are yet to come!

Endeavor: Let us look forward in reassurance knowing that Jesus answers prayers of all people and cares for all of His children in the world.

Prayer: Help us, Lord, to cry out in Jesus' name, thanks for the Covid vaccination You bring to healing our people and the multitude of people…doctors, nurses, and other medical workers in our lives. We thank God for the reminder of the scriptures as they relate to the Beatitudes and only pray that they become useful for our souls' salvation. Amen.

SACRIFICE

(Destruction or Surrender of Something
for the Sake of Something Else)

GREATER DAYS

*Who comforteth us in all our tribulation, that we may
be able to comfort them which are in any trouble, by the
comfort wherewith we ourselves are comforted of God.*

II CORINTHIANS 1:4

Mothers, fathers, siblings, teachers, neighbors, nurses, and ministers are some of the many great people who come forth in our sorrows to comfort and reassure us that the future will once again be bright and filled with hope despite our grievances and losses currently being physically or spiritually challenging. Generally, such physical experiences are naturally occurring and/or recurring such as growth and development, puberty, fracturing a limb, pulling a muscle, growing older or elderly, aches and pains, losing teeth or possible hearing and/or memory losses.

In most cases, our family physicians or specialists can diagnose the problem or problems and assist us in attaining ultimate health, strength, and rigor through physical and occupational therapies and daily exercise to restore us back to our previous statures and demeanors. Thus, provide comfort in our time of need as most certainly, we need all of the medical help and restoration which we can possibly receive to overcome our obstacles.

Dementia, Post-Traumatic Stress Disorder, amnesia and other psychologically and or neurologically-based disorders certainly can put undue stress upon an individual and his or her family in different ways but we can become comforted through the aid of licensed therapists, psychologists, and psychiatrists. We thank God by which He aids us in the out-pouring of His love, compassion, and humility through essential service workers such as all of those above mentioned.

Others, such as Mother Teresa, Saint Teresa of Calcutta who was an Albanian-Indian Roman Catholic nun and missionary who ministered to lepers, the homeless, and poorest of the poor in her love, devotion, and charity to the least of humanity albeit through God. He took care of her physical and mental health needs via all the years of her calling to aid, care, and comfort the most unfortunate and disenfranchised in society.

Do we sometimes lose sight of our blessings given us from the Lord? Wouldn't it be greater days if we could just show more humility and outreach toward others before ourselves? How about letting go and allowing God to do His great work in us? Can we then be trusted to perform the works of God's great disciples in our daily interactions with others?

Revelation: May we continuously work towards being mindful of other's needs.

Endeavor: Let us as a people lift our sights toward greater days in giving and sharing God's love.

Prayer: Help us to become beacons of divine healing in Jesus' name learning the teachings and love for which Mother Teresa had for her fellow man, woman, and child we pray knowing that God's works are not done in vain. Amen.

A LIGHTER MEANING

A man's heart deviseth his way: but
the Lord directeth his steps.

PROVERBS 16:9

The above scripture can only reign true if one stand's fast, holding onto the Lord's hand; with the Lord then allowed to direct one's steps. God allows us the choice to make decisions in our lives and live with the consequences of those choices "as a man's heart deviseth his way." But this must include permitting the Lord to direct our steps in how He wants His servants to be revealed to us on earth as in heaven. In all ways we must acknowledge Him (Proverbs 3:6). We must be ably ready to give Him the honor and the glory.

This makes me think of all the times in our lives when we hold on to far too much stuff which needs to be cleaned out of our homes or storage rooms, but we continue to hold onto it forever as I speak of myself for being a procrastinator in this area. Then as the old adage says, "One man's junk becomes another man's treasure." After finally selling, donating, or throwing stuff away in the garbage, we resolve to accept the fact that we no longer needed it to the point of even having it to begin with in our possessions.

Just wasted money from our banking accounts! All of which gave a lighter meaning to the above verse becoming active in our daily lives. Absolutely, it did not burn a hole into our pockets to rid ourselves of our junk as someone else needed it possibly more than us. Nor, did such a decision deflect from the Lord's steps. Therefore, my heart was left faultless in my desire to let it go as God was there to clean the mess up. Thank you, Jesus!

Now, it is also true that the Lord gives us a mind to reason and a heart to care. Mentally and physically, both systems must work together hand in hand, one with the other. Because oftentimes, what we think and how we think about a matter or circumstance, will determine the way in which we outwardly act in our hearts even in the smallest of matters. So, this process must be coveted in God or it becomes man's way and not directed by the Lord's steps.

Something to wonder about is our ability to communicate with our Lord. Do we actively ask Him to help and direct our steps or do we just assume that it is His job to do so? Can we surrender our ways and hearts for the betterment of the Lord's ways in our lives? Might we in the long run, make healthier and wiser decisions with God's direction and help?

Revelation: We can enable the Lord to direct His steps in our lives. Be submissive to the Lord in all things.

Endeavor: Allow us to know and remember that we can make choices pleasing to you.

Prayer: In a lighter meaning to the word of God, we must become submissive and make the needed sacrifices to be pleasing as servants of God. We certainly have been given the will to make the choice. It's simply up to us to do His will. Amen.

BUSTLING HOLIDAYS

To everything there is a season, and a time
to every purpose under the heaven.

ECCLESIASTES 3:1

Among the holidays, most people find themselves bustling from this place to that as they acquire the needed foods, candies, drinks, outdoor displays, and costumes for that particular holiday or season. There tends to be great joy with childhood innocence (even as experienced by adults) and sometimes mixed with anxiousness or a bit of depression as many families may be feeling overwhelmed by the frenzy of the holiday seasons.

From celebrating the beginning of the new year and welcoming in its designated slot of celebration… jumpstarts our personal efforts to make for living healthier lifestyles. Making bold and oftentimes, failed resolutions to lose weight, quit smoking or drinking alcoholic beverages, seek and follow our doctor's orders of maintaining a regular exercise program, cutting down on the fats and carbohydrates we intake in our diets and eating more fruits and vegetables, to drinking eight glasses of water per day to help purify and purge ourselves of intoxicants in our bodies.

Depending upon our religious beliefs, cultures, ethnicities, and forms of celebrations; we may say yes or no to proceed forth in the extraordinary festivities and activities planned throughout the year. There's Hanukkah, a Jewish holiday or Kwanzaa, an African celebration…both in which a culture celebrates its religious and or cultural values or both. On Valentine's Day one can be wined and dined and receive that gorgeous bouquet of flowers and box of chocolates from their loved ones.

Or during St. Patrick's Day, celebrating the luck of the Irish can prevail in eating corned beef, cabbage, and stew. On Good Friday or that Saturday before Easter Sunday, many times, families help to color hard-boiled eggs prior to the Easter egg hunt and the bunny arriving, then going to their respective religious services; then home or other relatives' homes to eat dinner.

There are celebrations for both Mother's and Father's Days, along with Memorial Day, family reunions and dinners with The Fourth of July fireworks and barbecues in between. Then comes Halloween and trick or treating and counting and eating our candies, to then, cooking and eating our Thanksgiving family dinner, and on Christmas Day exchanging gifts with family and friends before eating large again.

Therefore, in all things or every purpose there is a designated time or season under the heaven that God hath made beautiful in His time which no man can fully unravel from its beginning to ending. For there is a time for all things from births to deaths, war and peace, love and hate and so forth to exist and function. There is absolutely nothing new under the sun that God Himself has not ordained within the world that has happened.

Ask yourselves, just how often do we acknowledge the divine glory and presence of our Lord in daily living? In the hustle and bustle of our holidays and/or special occasions, do we include our Heavenly Father in the picture? Can we even remember or recall all the ways in which God has provided for our mere enjoyment and comfort? Do we praise Him enough for all of His blessings and are we sometimes even taking our breaths for granted?

Revelation: We can enjoy our bustling holidays and festivities for such times as these.

Endeavor: To enjoy everything that God has put before us on earth.

Prayer: Help us, Lord, to keep Your scriptures in the fore front of our lives. Remind us as You often do ever so lightly, the goodness and blessings of our days as You have provided for every purpose and season under the sun. Amen.

AT THE RIVER'S EDGE

And the woman conceived, and bare a son: and when she saw him that he was a goodly child, she hid him three months. And when she could no longer hide him, she took for him an ark of bulrushes. And daubed it with slime and with pitch, and put the child therein; and she laid it in the flags by the river's brink.

EXODUS 2:3

It appears that the woman was a Levite as well as her husband, meaning they were Hebrews which presented a problem for the Pharaoh who had placed a bounty on the head of each Hebrew boy being born to be killed immediately per his proclamation or decree. Why? Because Pharaoh wanted to control the destiny of the Hebrew people by placing them into bondage unto him as descendants of Israel. He felt that they might become too powerful.

No Hebrew boy was considered free from such atrocity; only predestined unto death by being thrown into the Nile River to drown. Therefore, the boy's mother, Jochebed decided otherwise for her son and took a chance by hiding him in a waterproofed basket with cattails and the like to be hidden in the reeds at the river's edge. Hopefully, he would soon be found one day by the Pharaoh's daughter who would be bathing in the river. Steps that she would take afterwards would certainly be crucial to the boy's life and future.

As the story proceeds, the Pharaoh's daughter decides to keep the baby and adopt him, naming him Moses because he was drawn from the water. She then becomes highly swayed by Miriam who just happened to be Moses' sister standing close by and overseeing everything to find a Hebrew mother to nurse Moses. In turn, Jochebed is chosen as a paid nurse maid and all that she had planned, worked out through Moses' life. It is assumed that Pharaoh accepted Moses as his grandson as he grew into adulthood as the Pharaoh's daughter's son and was never slain.

Why Moses was allowed to live and thrive among Pharaoh's people is never revealed in the Bible. Possibly, he excused the one Hebrew's death for the glory he might bring him in power or strength. Or possibly, he allowed such an act because of the compassion and devotion which his daughter had shown Moses and her want for him to live. No matter what the case, Moses escaped a predestined death. Otherwise, he may not have come upon such fortune in his young life as was manipulated by his mother.

Certainly, the old saying, "There's nothing as strong as the love of a mother for her child" speaks multitudes with Jochebed's love for Moses. Think of it, while most other Hebrew boys' lives were just taken at birth, who would believe the odds of survival of even one child because of the law of the land during that time? Most assuredly, God had great plans for Moses yet to be revealed during his tenure on earth and I'm sure much greater than his mother Jochebed ever imagined!

All of this goes to prove that none of us really know whom we shall encounter in our lifetimes and how they will either help or harm us. Nor what our tasks and trials shall be. We can only pray for the best and believe that God will send His loving angels to surround us and protect us with His loving armor in whatever destinations our lives take. But how many of us can honestly say that we prostrate ourselves before the Lord and allow Him to direct and guide our thoughts, decisions, and actions?

How hard would it be to just let God take control and decide our paths for which we should take? Imagine being a Jochebed and making such decisions not knowing the outcome, but depending upon a higher power which I believe that she did when she made her sacrifice. I also believe that she heard the words of God to take the steps which she did to ensure the life of Moses which beckons me to ask, "How often do we surrender all to Christ Jesus?"

Even if we found out that we had been given up at birth for adoption, might that be a change-agent in our willingness to follow the precepts of God, our Heavenly Father feeling that we really weren't wanted by our mother or parents and what does life really have to offer us after all? Or would we be open to loving the mother, father, or parents and family which God gave to us and placed us with instead? Possibly, in the mix, we find that we can love anew or just love what we have and be thankful and joyous for that? Later finding our true descendants will come in due time we tell ourselves, as we know that God is listening to our pleas.

Revelation: Certainly, there is something breathtaking at a river's edge where things simply come alive in beauty, clarification, purification, and change in our lives.

Endeavor: Help us to remember to thank and forever love those who genuinely have given so much life to us every day.

Prayer: When we ponder our misfortunes in life at the river's edge like Jochebed, may we remember Jesus and how He died for our sins and renewal, making a sacrifice into new life for us with Him and His Father as we are never alone in our trials and journeying on earth. Amen.

SIGNALING AHEAD

And it shall come to pass, that when they make a long blast with the ram's horn, and when ye hear the sound of the trumpet, all the people shall shout with a great shout; and the wall of the city shall fall down flat, and the people shall ascend up every man straight before him.

JOSHUA 6:5

Certainly, during the wartimes in the Bible, militias had used various signals ahead of whatever military maneuver they had hoped to use and penetrate their planned effort of defeat against their enemy or region of concern. Whether that had been signaling involved and utilized during vast military efforts on land and sea, it was a condition that had to proceed the action taken.

Such was the case in Jericho of blowing the ram's horn, then all of the people shouting thus, the walls falling flat down to the ground. Or, as spoken in Numbers 10:9; "And if you go to war in your land against the enemy that oppresseth you, then ye shall blow an alarm with the trumpets; and ye shall be remembered before the Lord your God, and ye shall be saved from your enemies." If the people would have refused to do their part as required by God, then the walls of Jericho would not have fallen opening the living quarters of the enemy.

Also, in Judges 20: 38 it states, "Now there was an appointed sign between the men of Israel and the liers in wait, that they should make a great flame with smoke rise up out of the city." Therefore, signaling ahead or giving a signal ahead of war was required to alert the armies before their charge in duty and witness their efforts to defeat their enemies. Without such a signal, the army would have basically lay in wait possibly to their own demise sacrificing their lives without a cause.

The same holds true to human life. As such, if there is distress in the body functioning, most generally an alarm will blow whether that be a scream or shout piercing to the human ear which lets others know of the distress the person(s) are in at the time. Equally, it could result in silence or lack of functioning instead or as well. The goal would be to reach out for medical assistance and not wander doing nothing at all, thus sacrificing our own health wellness not watching or listening to the signals.

It would be a sign of the internal war which one was encountering in his or her own body that would be afflicting the individual at the time. So, often in order to hopefully reach the moment of peace, one has to encounter a battle to fight, through the sending of an alarm to then achieve the necessary resolution of the problem(s). Thank God for the channeling of the signals to our benefit. The thing is that we must be willing to listen and become obedient servants to His words and directions for our lives and futures.

Then again, regarding the human body, various signs and or symptoms can alert us to many diseases or disorders lying within as we fight our internal enemy or enemies. So, one can conclude that things which give off negative effects or charges blowing the ram's horn or igniting the flame can give or result in positive charges or effects defeating the enemy within as well. We must learn to let go and hear God. Many times, He speaks to us silently through things which we can visibly see, witness and attest to in our lives for the benefit of helping others and bringing them to Christ as He uses us as the conduit of a ram's horn or flame.

What can we conclude regarding the signals which God has made and ordained? Can one see the rationale for comparing the ram's horn as a signal with an alarm of distress going off in the human body? How often do we take notice of the alarms within our own health and either do something or nothing about them? Have we sacrificed our own health for the non-blowing of the horn alerting us to our human conditions? What wars will this then result in that we have to fight?

Revelation: The human body often sends signals which we deny but others see and tell us about.

Endeavor: May we welcome in the future our abilities to look for the signals which lie in wait in our bodies for attention to needed healthcare.

Prayer: Help us, Lord, to help others receive their signals with a gentler approach so as not to sacrifice their own health wellness. But in all fairness, God provides us individually with the needed signals in many cases to execute our own decisions for the good of our own welfare as well as others. Amen.

A SIGNING EVENT

And God spake all these words, saying I am the
Lord thy God, which have brought thee out of the
land of Egypt, out of the house of bondage.

EXODUS 20:2

On the day that God took His hand and wrote these words which I shall summarize shortly, He had come to the end of His journey in trying to turn the Israelites around in their relationship with Him. They had actually come to the point of idolizing false gods and turning away from the principles of the covenant which they had originally formed with God. There was no telling as to how this angered God and everything for which He stood.

As the people were stationed at the base of Mt. Sinai, Moses was called up the mountain by God to talk with Him. And as Moses stood silent honoring God and all that He stood for on sacred ground such as prophetic truth, justice, faith, and sacrifice, Moses listened as God allowed him to witness (be in His presence) while God's fingers were writing out the Ten Commandments right before his very eyes. It was the most important signing event of our Lord at that moment.

And all of the people saw and heard the roar of thunder and flash lightning with the mountain caught up in smoke. All of this activity seemed to disrupt the actions of the Israelites causing them to move out from where they stood and question what had happened atop the mountain. But God spoke to the people directing them in the ways that they should follow and perform certain activities to the glory of God and not worshipping false idols.

In paraphrasing the Ten Commandments as spoken and written by God, they read as follows: there are no other Gods but God above; no graven images should be made in heaven, on earth or beneath in the water, God is a jealous God and wants no one worshipping anyone or thing but Him, show mercy to others, love God and keep His commandments, never take the Lord, God's name in vain. Keep the Sabbath day (Sunday) Holy, only work six days but keep the Sabbath work-free, the seventh day is hallowed and blessed as the Lord rests.

Further, to live a longer life, one should honor one's parents and never do any of the following: kill (except if God commands), commit adultery, steal, bear false witness against one's neighbor or covet anything that is one's neighbor's in his or her household.

These were the ordered and spoken words of the Lord to His people. And they were to listen and apply these commandments in their own lives accordingly from that day forth. To do otherwise, they then sinned against God Himself and that could result in punishment to the people or person.

In those days, these commandments must have been pretty hard to think about, let alone follow but they now became the law of the land. I cannot imagine all of the unrest and upheaval which Moses had to endure with his people. People who already had been defiant, rebellious, difficult to lead and unmanageable. Now, his major task was to get them in line and follow the order of the commandments as a sacrifice to God.

How many of us reading this entry feel lost in the wilderness away from the commandments of the Lord? May I recommend that you get on your knees and pray to our Father or visit your house or a house of worship to help direct and guide your thoughts, footpaths, and actions as you embark upon a new understanding of what God says regarding His commandments. God does not want you to abandon ship. Rather, He wants us to learn to grow in grace in our understanding of His signed words engraved on the stone tablets, which the Israelites and us as followers of Christ continue to honor even today. What was said yesterday is good even until today, tomorrow and forever more.

Were there disruptions, confrontations, and possible assaults or wars? Did the Israelite people make reasonable allowances for the new changes which now infiltrated their camps? How many days did such changes take to persuade the Israelites in their new directions as set by God? Were there deserters to the conditions set forth in the commandments who just got lost in the wilderness all over again? How many survivors were there in all of the ruckus? Remember, God delivered the Israelites out of bondage making a sacrifice to them.

Revelation: Know that it is good to go back and review the words of the Ten Commandments to use in our daily lives.

Endeavor: May we endeavor to understand the sacrifices which were made to serve our Heavenly Father daily.

Prayer: Lord, help us to understand and follow Your words according to Your will and not ours. Please enable us to make the needed sacrifices to ourselves and others according to Your will be done on earth as it is in heaven as we grow in understanding and grace. Amen.

MR. MANDELA'S RISE
FOR FREEDOM

Freedom floats... subtlety;
as a butterfly spreading, gliding, and fluttering
its magnificently-colored and delicate wings...
which spread symmetrically apart and hover
gently in mid-air forming almost, closed palms...
praying dutifully in anticipation of its daily meals.
Freedom hovers, gently suckling the nectar's sweet juices!

Freedom speaks.... softly;
uttering secrets and mysteries learned from times past,
unveiled as whisperings of familiar melodies into our ears...
beating their native instruments spoken in foreign tongues;
heard throughout many lands, including my land of Africa...
resounding in its own right to tell everyone of its own truths.
Freedom flows, eloquently shaping the River Niger's mouth!

Freedom cries... hauntingly;
ailing our bodies, our minds, and our souls
reminding us to never forget Apartheid; remembering...
the many still suffering in bondage throughout the world today;

DONNA COLLIER RICKMAN

as Freedom does not simply jump right out of us unshackled…
rather, it tugs and pushes our souls; stinging our hearts forever.
Freedom beats… irregularly in uprooted, fleeting percussions!

Freedom celebrates… indiscriminately;
hollering and stomping and making itself known to all
volleying between oppression, degradation, and segregation…
watching us spew gut-wrenching feelings of jubilation,
felt in victorious liberations flowing throughout our limbs…
as seen from people of all nationalities, cultures, genders and ages.
Freedom dances… gracefully tickling the bare feet of our souls!

Freedom rises… briskly;
emerging from our country, motherland's roots flowing upward,
then and outward; releasing itself as iridescent beckoning lights…
rendering powerful, majestic rhythms and synchronized beats
permeating all that is, has been and forever shall be Free…
"like the lovely butterfly whose delicate wings pray in mid-air."
Freedom soars…elevating our once, broken and encased wings!

Freedom floats atop us… like a hovering butterfly,
Freedom speaks within us… singing sweet melodies,
Freedom cries unto us…in unsynchronized beats,
Freedom celebrates alongside us …dancing victoriously,
Freedom soars around us…awakening spiritual flights.

FREEDOM, FREEDOM, FREEDOM!
Mr. Mandela's Rise to Freedom!

Written by Donna Collier Rickman

STRENGTH

(Quality or State of Being Strong)

BENT LIKE THAT

"My flesh and my heart faileth; but God is the strength of my heart and my portion forever."

PSALM 73:26

My mother was born with and afflicted all of her life by a disorder called Sickle Cell Anemia. It is an inherited blood disease which affects the red blood cells and is caused by an oxygen insufficiency that makes the cells become misshapen and sickle like the curved farm tool blade. There can be many accompanying health ailments which in turn result as the blood vessels constrict and possibly clot, along with severe deterioration of the body tissues and bone marrow. Stroke and heart attack were just two debilitating disorders which could occur in her present condition.

In 1976, she underwent a failed surgery for a broken hip from a fall that became introverted. Several days following, my mother became hospitalized as she continually oozed blood from this wound and thus, received multiple blood transfusions in the interim. Momma never recovered, becoming comatose and eventually, bled to death from her hip several days later. She amassed much suffering and pain in her flesh throughout her life before finally being called home to Jesus at the young age of forty-four. Her flesh and heart faileth, but God was the source of her strength, heart and portion forever.

It seems that some things are just bent like that and nothing one can do can change the set of circumstances from whence they originated. Although I initially screamed and hollered and was probably in shock over her passing, I had to give all praise and glory to God who took her home. Throughout her life, she forever held unto the hand of the Lord as she listened for His still, soothing voice to direct her steps. Finally, welcoming His daughter home with open arms; she knew that while His eye stayed on the sparrow, He had been watching her all along as well.

Can we be so courageous and vigilant as to hold on to God's invisible hand for our strength in days on this earth in the midst of our suffering until the moment of our meeting Him in His arms? Can we speak God's name and have faith to believe He is our portion forever? Have we everlasting love and gratitude found in the precious name of our Lord for all that He has done and continues to do to guide and direct our lives? Can we listen for God's voice to tell us "Well done my good and faithful servant," for one's work done while on this earth? Certainly, a life well lived!

Revelation: Speak to the Lord and ask Him for comfort and resolve in our sufferings.

Endeavor: Know that God is our refuge and our strength upon Whom we can depend in our darkest moments.

Prayer: Dear Lord, hold us forever in Your loving arms so that we might feel Your arms of protection even when passing through the shadow of death. And for those who are witnesses to such a transition, may we be willing to tell the good news of the Lord in His carrying His child home to glory. Amen.

SEARING OVERFLOW

Fear thou not; For I am with thee: be not dismayed; for I am thy God: I will strengthen thee; yea, I will help thee; yea, I will uphold thee with the right hand of my righteousness.

ISAIAH 41:10

With the current Coronavirus pandemic cases in the United States closing in on almost 20 million and deaths surmounting to almost 344,000 (a horrendous searing overflow since the end of December 2020), it was no wonder that precautions were set in place by March 2020 when The Centers for Disease Control and the president sent our national economy into a blistering halt of uncertain functionality.

With Stay In Place (at home) sanctions set for all Americans being mandated into operation and instituted across the nation back in March; precautions set to frequently wash hands, wear gloves, masks or scarfs as protective face equipment and for our first responders (essential workers) to wear PPE equipment working with the general public.

In conjunction, all Americans are to follow the six-foot social distancing rule in open as well as closed places. All nonessential businesses were shut down until further notice following safety precautions. Such businesses included churches, gyms, restaurants, bakeries, daycares, all schools, nail and hair salons, and so forth.

God has told us not to become frightened or forlorn in our thoughts and actions for we are not alone and Him who is our head… walks and talks with us to strengthen us and bring us through the valley of the shadow of death. Coronavirus appeared out of the blue. I believe it can also, disappear just as quickly once a vaccine can be found. For God is our help in trouble felt on every side and He is our saving grace.

Certainly, not without the tools that God Himself has armed us with to protect ourselves by wearing the full armor will these mandates become effective. We must go to Him in prayer and become obedient to His word for our lives! Only in Him will we find refuge to defeat the viruses rampant in the United States. They have occurred before and been conquered or quelled, so most certainly, victory will prevail again!

We are not to fear, nor be dismayed for God is omnipresent and ready to respond, not react to whatever the problem or situation might be at hand. He will strengthen us and give us hope and a future. He will lead us out of the darkness into the light. He will direct our paths and provide a safe haven for us amidst the virulent chaos and uphold us with His right hand of righteousness.

Are we leaning on God and entrusting ourselves to His care? Or are we impatiently jumping on the sidelines looking for a quick fix? Do you believe that God will intervene and have the final say in this matter? There will be a calm in the storm. His Son, Jesus did it for Peter and the seamen and He'll do it for us even today. We will find restoration in the Lord. Do you believe that?

Revelation: Know that God is the Master in all things despite a searing overflow of disease.

Endeavor: Read the Bible daily for strength in the Lord; not powerlessness.

Prayer: Ask for His will to be revealed throughout the chaos as well as the calm. We must know and believe that God is with us, will comfort us, let us not be dismayed but feel strengthened by His love and care as Jesus sits on His right hand of righteousness as God upholds us. Amen.

MOUNT THEM UP

But they that wait upon the Lord shall renew their strength;
they shall mount up with wings as eagles; they shall run,
and not be weary; and they shall walk, and not faint.

ISAIAH 40:31

In determining God's greatness, mercy, majesty, and adoration, there has never been and will never be one to match His equal. Lucifer tried but look at all of the gaps regarding God's creation in the beginnings that were missed, overlooked, and forgotten otherwise by him a fallen angel. Lucifer known as Satan would certainly try to break through any and all snares of God's prophets that carry God's messages and disciples that followed Jesus then and most certainly, now in His teachings within this modern age because that is his job to roam the earth to and from one place to another and do just that.

Only God knew the missing details to put the parts of the puzzle together in solving man and woman's place on earth, within the universe, and beyond on the moon or down below in the sea. Man has certainly tried to solve all of the mazes in this matter called existence, however, even in all of the finds of research regarding medicine, technology, human growth and development, disease, agism, and the like... no one still will know it all above God.

Thinking of the eagle, it is known to have one of the largest wingspans on earth of about over 8 feet. They are our saluted bird in American society exemplifying the courage, strength, agility, majesty, honor, grace, and protection, for which they fly and exist. We base our patriotism to the flag analogous to the eagle flying high to freedom as a freed bird graced on the horizon. Just think of how esteemed it must be amongst bird species and is noted in the Bible many times over.

I liken the part of the above verse, "They that wait upon the Lord shall renew their strength; they shall mount up with wings as eagles" to men and women in the military mounting up into their armor and being on the battlefield for our Lord. They shall persevere whether running or walking and thus, not become weary or faint in the process. And this is what we as individuals will need to do to fight in God's great army of life. We must hold fast and stay focused on our tasks at hand to avoid defeat by the enemy and stay strengthened!

God is there for us and will not let us stay fallen forever if that is what it comes to. We will rise up and soar again above the mountains and the clouds drawing our wings like eagles to renew our strength. We shall forever walk and run tall and proud like within the military and be a beacon of hope for all those who have become weary and faint of heart.

Have you ever felt God's almighty strength like that of an eagle? How many of you liken an eagle to majesty displaying God's omnipotence? And when you have mounted up, have you felt renewed in energy and spirit?

Revelation: Let us remember to feel as free-spirited as the eagle.

Endeavor: May we not forget our wings of protection given from the Lord.

Prayer: Help us, Lord, to look on high to the mighty eagle for strength to walk with uplifted arms and hands, to knock down barriers with our talons, to seek refuge flying high in the air like a trapeze artist in the Lord's word. And most importantly, to wait upon the Lord to renew our strength. Amen.

FALLING RIGHTEOUSLY

Many are the afflictions of the righteous: but the
Lord delivereth him out of them all. He keepeth
all his bones: not one of them is broken.

PSALM 34:19, 20

Anyone who has ever fallen, and that is most everyone from child to adult has probably had to do a double-take first asking him or herself, "What just happened?" or "Did that really happen to me?" Yes, it did and that is why you're on the floor or the ground. Sometimes, I have actually witnessed small children ages 2-5 question themselves about their incidents to the point of almost reenacting their falls all over again as they're so bewildered and a bit flustered regarding the whole thing.

Luckily and in most cases, people, especially children have totally recovered from roll-overs, side splits, flips, slips and the like. Possibly, they could have become performance artists flying through the air with the greatest of ease with not a single muscle contusion or broken bone to be found. However, as a person grows older, so do the risks increase with falls. I'm a witness to numerous experiences in various locations which resulted in many afflictions as the Lord delivered me out of them all minus any broken bones.

I'll never forget rolling down our basement steps as a young girl age 3-6 and would continually pick myself up, dust myself off and commence rolling again until I had had enough of the churning motion associated with it in my tummy and the tingling feeling all over my body. Talking about resilience, strength, and fun times, I had it! So, I felt very well prepared for plunges or the need to fall over later in life…so to speak. However, over time such illusions became a mixed bag of injuries and pain.

I've had the usual childhood falls from jump roping, relay races, and jumping from a moving swing. But then came adulthood; into my twenties, thirties, forties, fifties, and sixties as changes came in and to my body as I reflect. One time when I was seven months pregnant, our family cat challenged me by taking one of my fried chicken legs from off a plate on my kitchen countertop. Literally, it had me chasing her up the stairs in our duplex whereby, I stumbled up some steps but luckily had no medical mishap…just a few scrapes to my hand and an ailing leg.

Another time, I missed the top of a ledge of porch stairs being in a hurry to walk outdoors and tripped plummeting to the ground. This resulted in my wearing a sling on one arm and a leg boot or immobilizer because of muscle twisting and injury. Even still, I had a situation at my house in which upon my walking unto the top stair of my porch outdoors, slid all the way down sideways landing unto our concrete sidewalk as there was black ice there. With one leg bent underneath me and an arm behind me, I distinctly recall hitting every step with the full force of my body. Literally, I dragged my whole body back up to the house using my rail. Thank God for the strength of my upper body. No one had seen me, so could anyone help me? No, not at all!

I remember going to work that day and they wanted to take me to the emergency room, which I should have just gone on to the hospital in the first place. All for my so-called dedication to teaching, as the pain and suffering won over. It ended up that I had suffered multiple contusions over my body and had pulled hip and back muscles. I was out of work almost four days plus the weekend in recovery.

Another quirky kind of fall happened to my disfavor one day when I was at work teaching and decided to skip across a parking lot between curbs with about three of my students. Suddenly, I was miss-stepping upon the curb's sidewalk and instead, tripped and fell down upon my right shoulder. I knew something was amiss because I could barely move the arm. After about three months of physical therapy and ultrasound imaging, I found out that I had actually suffered a right shoulder rotator cuff tear far into the muscle. It required major surgery for tissue repair and over six weeks in full recovery and therapy to heal. Although no bones were broken, thank you Lord... I always felt like my arm was literally hanging by its ligaments and tendons. For months, it felt not totally connected somehow and ached precariously at the least movement.

Then there was the time in which I took my grandchildren to the bowling alley. They were ages 3, 7, and 10. We put our shoes on and walked over to the bowling lanes. The officials had placed a metal contraption in front to help the younger ones to hopefully roll the ball down the middle of the lane, not becoming gutter balls. All seemed well until a grandson's arm decided to throw a ball versus roll a ball toward the next lane. Watching, I decided that I needed to retrieve it so as no one might otherwise get hurt.

So, instead of my catching it, I essentially fell backwards after sliding on one of my legs which bent behind me and hit the lane thigh first. Following, I found myself still sliding into the lane in all kinds of positions until three helpers came. I couldn't even stand up again without their assistance as they walked in the gutters, I believe handing me a metal tool to hold unto to walk off the greased lane. Luckily, I recovered before leaving the alley and could actually bowl again with a minimum of pain. Later that evening and since then, I do have relapses of pain that radiate throughout the leg.

And still another episode recently occurred when I had left a fund-raising event at a local college and tripped over some pavement which was uneven in their walkway. I literally just missed falling headfirst unto the pavement as one leg was twisted outward while my arm was flung in front of me protecting my face as I tried to cover my fall. I remember looking for someone to just help me to my feet but to no avail... no one came forth. Again, luckily no bones had been broken and the Lord had covered me with His wings of protection as I stood up and walked away trusting in His strength.

Possibly, my early training rolling down the stairs had afforded me some aversion to even greater dangers. In any event, I thanked the Lord each time for full recovery from all of my falls. I certainly pray for no more such falls and feel blessed that the Lord has felt me righteous enough as a servant of His to come forth through my afflictions. Hence, with no broken bones.

How often do we look for the Lord at the heart of our afflictions? When falling, if you've not experienced any broken bones, do you count yourself as lucky or blessed? And what can one discern from all of the falls one has experienced in one's life… if any? Possibly, that the Lord has blessed you with some pretty good bones. Hard, strong and solid!

Revelation: May we remember that in all of our afflictions, the Lord does provide us protection as we place our strength in Him.

Endeavor: Allow us to come to know the favor for which the Lord has for His righteous servants.

Prayer: Help us, Lord, to thank you for coming forth to rescue us in our trials such as falling righteously that we are delivered through our adversities to the point of not breaking even one bone. Amen.

TRUST

(One in which confidence is placed)

IDOL WORSHIP

*"Confounded be all they that serve graven images, that
boast themselves of idols; worship Him all ye Gods."*

PSALM 97:7

Certainly, with gaming and all of the techy devices such as tablets,
laptops, smart phones and video gaming systems imbedded within our
society today, it seems that very little time is actually given unto the
Lord. But is deep concerted prayer and listening for our Father's voice
in terms of true worship, honor, and Holy Godliness afforded to Him
by today's standards? Or have we simply put our trust into other gods?
Gods which we would die without or at least be lost to and feel doomed
in our family, financial, and workplace situations and futures.

And what about all of the other eminently carved and crafted
sports and achievement awards generally handed out to sports figures,
Hollywood stars, and pure geniuses annually; they can leave us with a
world filled with idols being things and people whom we grandiosely
adore if not... fall in love with and honor many times over before the
Lord. Just how much have we entrusted others before the Lord, our God?

And the people in the world would probably admonish us saying,
"This is the way of our world...man's way!" Some might even ask the
question, "And what exactly did God have to do with it and the running
of it?" Everything seemingly then built, manufactured, produced,
installed, and functioning only because of the will and domain of man
alone? Man might only believe what he hears and sees as evidence only
regarding the evolution of things in this world.

But what does the Lord say in His commandment? "Thou shalt not have any other Gods before me." This is the standard, the law, and the way in which we should live standing upon the promises of God and His words in the Bible. Not what mere man or woman pronounces, punctuates, and proclaims but what does the Bible say? Maybe, we need to revisit and read its passages more often and more clearly, brothers and sisters in Christ, preferably on a daily basis.

One might ask what does the Bible have to do with the world and all that goes on it? It was written from the inspired words of God Himself for man to first believe without any doubt the teachings as set forth for man and woman to follow accordingly. But because of "free will' God gives us that liberty to choose what it is that we believe our truths, rights, judgements, and consequences of our thoughts and actions, and worship to be...whether God, the Father or idols.

So, I ask you sisters and brothers, is it any wonder that men and women put such grave emphasis upon these idols and images? Do such things as idols and graven images control our thinking (mindset), self-esteem, confidence and rationale for living? What would happen if for some reason, they became obsolete? Who would people gravitate toward then and for how long? Until the next greatest idol or image came along which would save them from what? Or would they remember Christ first as their Savior?

Revelation: Live only for Christ today, tomorrow, and forever.

Endeavor: Oh Lord, help us to remain faithful and honorable to You, putting only You first in our lives.

Prayer: May we remember to not put anything before God's commandment. Help us to choose and remain faithful to Your words dear Heavenly Father versus those in the world and through the help of the Serenity Prayer...come to know the difference. Amen.

WRITING GINGERLY

Trust in the Lord with all thine heart and
lean not unto your own understanding.

PROVERBS 3:5

In my salutations to book editors, I try very intentionally to correctly write their names and titles attentively addressed before my written cover or query letter in hopes of securing a read manuscript.

Now, some may ask, "What does formality and correctness have to do with "trusting in the Lord with all thine heart and leaning not toward one's own understanding" in the manuscript? Well, in the world of writing, the two go hand in hand. Certainly, correctness takes into account all content and semantics in the cover or query letter but does not God take umbrage to our own understanding of what He has in store for our lives as writers in the full and completed manuscript if but we trust upon His word?

We can all hope for what we want regarding what we believe the editor will evoke from our earnest stories and/or writings for the reader, however if we trust not in God then our dreams for publishing may become a forlorn thought placed into a slush pile of wannabe's.

We must write gingerly and proceed with resolve to not place our heart in the thicket of our manuscript, becoming overly-anxious or frustrated in what we believe are found in the desires of our hearts as writers. We must go further to delineate the message of truth which has been given us as writers to convey to our audience from the Lord as we trust in Him to lead and guide us.

This thing called trust in God must be a standard for which we lean on wholeheartedly, not haphazardly. It is leaning on the Lord with our whole heart, soul, and mind that He will not leave us in the fray. Allow Him to pick up our thoughts and utterances transferred to writings for others to digest, yet not still thirst and hunger for the truth in His word.

When was the last time you trusted in God wholeheartedly? Can we become filled with His word when meditating upon the Lord for our subsistence? Does or can writing be a form of simple deliverance from drudgery in everyday life? Think on it and listen for what you hear in responses to then write the truth as purged from your being.

Revelation: Seek God and you shall find His truth in your writings.

Endeavor: Seek God sooner than later in one's writing process to guarantee a final published product.

Prayer: Trust in God's word, not one's own for understanding. For times caught sulking in the muck for a better word than procrastinating and losing one's muse, just take some time out away from the keyboards and reexamine your purpose for writing and publishing and to whom. What do you hope to achieve and for what in the process? Amen.

SHORT-TAILED FEATHERS

And he (Noah) stayed yet other seven days; and again, he
sent forth the dove out of the ark; And the dove came in
to him in the evening; and, lo, in her mouth was an olive leaf
pluckt off so Noah knew that the waters were abated from
off the earth. And he stayed yet other seven days; and sent
forth the dove; which returned not again unto him anymore.

GENESIS 8:10-12

Short-tailed feathered birds are known for their ability to fly in and out
of smaller spaces and situations skirting danger that surrounds them. It
is also known and can be viewed by the public as to how they manage
their flight patterns through the air and spaces based on the shortness of
their feathers. Feathers are well known to provide warmth, protection,
and establish mating patterns in the bird world also, depending upon
their colors.

In particular, the dove which Noah sent three times after the flood
to test the height of the waters was noted for its ability to instinctively
do what Noah had wanted it to do, then persevere and fly back to the
Ark with a report to Noah of no dry earth or near dry earth for man
and creatures including the fowl, beasts, reptiles, and amphibians to be
set free.

With the nip of its beak or bite from its mouth, the dove was able to
bring an olive leaf which it plucked off from its stem back to Noah. It
was divinely planned that such a task would be that of the dove sent as
a messenger of God's revelation to Noah. Through Noah's obedience,

discipline, and trust in God, he had followed through to complete the construction and building of the Ark to begin with and collecting two of every species to board it prior to the flood all over the earth.

Ironically, although Noah had witnessed this olive leaf which was a surefire sign of waters which had abated the earth brought back by the dove, he still sent the dove back a third time. With the dove not returning, this must have solidified the decision which Noah had made to release everything upon the Ark unto safe grounds and or waters. Possibly, he had heard the voice of God assuring him equally that the earth was indeed dry ground.

In any event, the Bible showcased the importance and work of the dove in this book of Noah which lets mankind know how necessary and important the functioning of the bird really was. It could easily fly between high and low places, between spaces, and land on high ground in fields for a look out. I am surprised that Noah did not send the pair of doves out together since one was left aboard the Ark afterwards. They probably found each other in the air and formed a family as did the other couples who departed.

What a time it must have been for Noah and his family as well in the midst of witnessing all the happenings going on and feeding the species of creatures aboard the Ark. I am still so amazed at the number of non-believers who did not board the Ark. According to scripture, their demise was left in the floods as well as all other creatures who could not board the Ark which was the world as it was known then.

In times like these, if a vaccine made itself available to mankind for the Coronavirus, how many would believe that it was a gift from God Himself above and would take it? Or how many would doubt that such a miracle antidote could exist in light of the numbers of deaths and contractions and thus opt out? Do we truly trust the words of God in the Bible and His actions for our sakes or take them only for lost words of the past?

Revelation: Realize that there are connections which happened in the Bible which are forever relevant and present in our world today.

Endeavor: Enable us to make wiser decisions based upon Your words of yesterday, today, tomorrow, and forever.

Prayer: Lord, give us the trust, wisdom, fortitude, and obedience to draw upon Your promises as had Noah. Enlighten our hearts to the importance for which short-tailed birds such as the dove play in our panoramic view of the world which surrounds us and brightens our days. Amen.

CASTING ONE'S CARES

Fret not thyself because of evildoers, neither be thou envious against the workers of iniquity. For they shall soon be cut down like the grass, and wither as the green herb. Trust in the Lord, and do good; so shalt thou dwell in the land, and verily thou shalt be fed. Delight thyself also in the Lord; and he shall give thee the desires of thine heart. Commit thy way unto the Lord; trust also in Him; and He shall bring it to pass.

PSALM 37: 1-5

There seems to be so much treachery, divisiveness, chaos, bias, envy, and downright evil witnessed in our nation and world today. For all that it took for God to form, build, and design the world's nations based on His images of what they should look like, act like and behold, it seems a disgrace these days for how they are currently functioning. Certainly, not as God had planned, intended and foreshadowed, I am sure.

As God has allowed Satan to roam from this place and that all over the world, touching this culture of people and that, it is no wonder that there are so many evildoers… those who have chosen to not follow the light, footsteps, and teachings of our Father in heaven and His son, Jesus Christ to work in iniquity and sin in their daily lives.

During the days when Jesus was born and later walked the earth, King Herod wanted to take His life and those of the Jewish boys. He did not know Jesus…what He looked like but had heard about Him and did not want to encounter Him and all of the power given Him from the Holy Father. King Herod was known for killing others, those he despised or felt threatened by at a moment's notice.

He was so evil that at one point, he had John the Baptist who baptized Jesus beheaded. What does that say about the character of the individual? In his last days, it has been noted by a scientific researcher that King Herod suffered tremendous pain and symptoms associated with various organs in his body resulting in a painful death.

And as noted above in the scriptures, King Herod was cut down as the grass and withered quickly as the green herb. We have to be conscious of the choices which we make in life and how they might affect not only others but us individually in our soul's salvation. It seems obvious that King Herod cared little about his life after death and what consequences his actions would reap in the afterlife in heaven.

Much is the same today for rulers over Third World nations and the effects of their rule over their regions. There are killings of all sorts of nature in and because of cultural and religious divides; sex trafficking and slavery amongst very young girls, not yet women; multitudes of immigrants seeking asylum in the United States, and a continuum of socioeconomic problems facing nations such as ours.

Again, all of this is certainly not what God had planted in His Eden with Adam and Eve here on earth as people began more and more worshipping and idolizing structures and things not of God in a modern-day Sodom and Gomorrah. We as a nation, need to open our Bibles to read that the past is presently upon us and becoming our future if we do not lean upon and seek the knowledge, understanding, and wisdom of the Lord. We need to cast our cares upon the Lord.

We are to trust and delight ourselves in the Lord so that we might do good and dwell in the house of the Lord forever more and relying upon our being fed His food for our sustenance in His kingdom. If we but commit our lives unto God, He will then give us the desires, well-intended, healthy, and good for our lives here on earth. He will provide us our daily bread and make allowances for us in areas which we fall short in for His benefit.

How many of us can say that we truly cast our worries upon the Lord? Do we pray daily and open the scriptures to our concerns or just lean upon our own understandings in the world in which we live?

How many of us can attest the horror of a King Herod in our lives today? Have socioeconomic times made a divide between our spiritual relationship we have had with Jesus or can we count Him as our Lord and Savior?

Endeavor: Let us learn to trust the teachings of our Heavenly Father leaning upon Him in our daily living.

Revelation: May we learn to cast our cares upon Jesus as He stands on the Father's words.

Prayer: Allow us to pray for the King Herod's of today that they find God, then be rewarded total deliverance in the sanctity of His words. We must all from time to time remember the words not to fret thyself because of evildoers, as God will handle them. Amen.

WISDOM

(Ability to discern inner
qualities and relationships)

GLORIOUS PRINCIPLES

The discretion of a man deferreth his anger; and
it is his glory to pass over a transgression.

PROVERBS 19:11

Many times, in our day to day living, we may become overwhelmed in an argument or disagreement with a family member, friend, co-worker, associate or someone who is a complete stranger that happened to enter our lives at a very unique time and place when our guards are down and we're more likely to become enraged versus ignore the situation at hand altogether. Glory be to God!

And even though your initial encounter was non-threatening, you suddenly find yourself in a completely different place... in affect, in attitude, in personality and in sound mind. As a matter of fact, throughout the entire encounter, you almost feel that your mind has left your body and you wonder, "Who's left standing there arguing in the midst of everything..." until you realize, it is simply you!

Sometimes, we are targeted and become the victimized, the shunned, the disenfranchised and criticized ones who become preyed upon, jumped on and our very movements silenced into existence by those who feel the need to overpower, dominate and subjugate those around them. This may leave us feeling less than worthy of God's grace, mercy, dominion and glory in this world. We have to remember that all power is in our hands, bodies, minds, and souls and the victory is ours if we remain with our eyes fixed upon the Lord in all of His wisdom.

It is then that we have to revisit the glorious principles of God in the living Bible such as long-suffering, patience, virtue, righteousness, praise, love, hope, faith, tolerance and forgiveness. In times of confrontation and indignation, we need our internal mechanisms of discretion to help us to remember these principles in our hearts, bodies, minds, and souls. No matter what a man or woman does against our person, we must remember that Jesus died for our sins and theirs that we all might have everlasting life. Nothing is so pressing to carry such angst against one's brother or sister.

Are you willing and ready to reject Satan and all of his imps and pitfalls which can lead us away from the glory of Jesus Christ, God and the Holy Spirit? Can you truly testify to the greatness of the Lord? Which of the glorious principles are you lacking to embolden you and follow such principles?

Revelation: Help us to keep our minds stayed upon God, our Lord in all of His wisdom.

Endeavor: Know that we embody the glorious principles of our Heavenly Father, so use them.

Prayer: Forgive us and deliver us, Father, from our daily transgressions so that Your children may be seen as acceptable in Your sight oh Lord, we do pray. And in areas where we fall short and miss the marks for salvation, enlighten us and allow us to cast our burdens upon You. Amen.

AN OLD SOUL

My son, if thou wilt receive my words, and hide my commandments
with thee; so that thou incline thine ear unto wisdom, and apply
thine heart to understanding; yea, if thou criest after knowledge,
and liftest up thy voice for understanding; For the Lord giveth
wisdom: out of His mouth cometh knowledge and understanding.

PROVERBS 2:1-3; 2:6

I cannot tell you how often I heard growing up about particular
members within the African-American communities within Hannibal,
Missouri, who were afforded a particular title. He or she was actually
seen, admired, recognized, and schooled as an old soul. This person was
deemed such that he or she had earned any and all of his or her stripes
as an individual with the blessed goodness, honor, praise, and most
important characteristic of living; wisdom.

He or she could be known as a localized guru and/or griot within his
or her family as well. He or she or both, many times had had a thorough
and working knowledge of the Heavenly Father, Son, and Holy Spirit
(Trinity) and Bible that was used in one's life as well as others. Therefore,
as is written in the above verses, cries out for knowledge and lifts up
one's voice for understanding within their own hearts as well as others.

And upon all the living that each had been able to do with their added
giftedness to experience and share with their families, community, and
others who would ever sit or stand and listen… to their greatness. Can't
you see them now and hear their words of wisdom as exalted within
their very beings? How did they become so filled and knowledgeable in

life? Was it simply a gift given them from our Father above? And were they somehow or another acting as a conduit for the Lord?

The simplest of words which they would even speak made such an enormous impact upon others that they would many times be spoken about as having an old soul. Such characteristics which linked them to the many years behind their births, but connected them equally, to the many years still remaining before them which time could never take away, but only enhance others' understanding of the greater meanings in life.

Many times, they could be dubbed as that old soul even though maybe he or she wasn't so old in years but just showcased a way about oneself to be categorized that way. There have been times when I was labeled as having had an old soul about me and I was a younger woman. Giving much thought to such a title made me think if God's presence in my life has been about me spreading truths about what has already happened or is yet to come as well in others' lives.

And in all things, one would need to have the understanding and hide the commandments within one's heart to get to the wisdom of the matter at hand. Has there been a time that you thought you were part of a bigger picture and had so much wisdom to impart to others that maybe, you didn't know what to do with it? How did you act and what did you do? Did you share it with others or just keep it locked within your very soul? Have you ever wondered what God's role was in this part of your life... being an old soul?

Revelation: Accept the fact that you may have been given a bigger task in this life to impart your knowledge and understandings unto others while keeping the commandments at hand.

Endeavor: When crying out for understanding, expect that God will deliver, providing you knowledge in the interim as you await the wisdom yet to come forth in your life and others.

Prayer: Ask God for discernment or sensitivity in your understanding of the wisdom which you have been given. And in all of our ways according to God's words ...we should get wisdom and understanding to then pass on to others in our daily interactions. Amen.

A LITTLE WHILE LONGER

I will instruct thee and teach thee in the way in which thou shat go: I will guide thee with mine eye.

PSALM 32:8

Just as Ruth who lost her husband onto death and Naomi who lost both her sons unto death, they both listened to that still small voice of God. Naomi was initially going to sojourn alone but heard God ask her to ask her daughters in law to go with her as mother-in- law to live and work in her country with her people; thus, not return to their own. That is exactly what Ruth did as the other daughter in law, Orpah refused and went back to her land and people.

The story continues on to reflect just how Naomi then directed Ruth in her daily work until her meeting with Boaz to the point of their eventual marital union in the Lord. Again, had Ruth not listened to the word which Naomi received from the Lord, then they both would not have been fruitful in their blessings from the Father. Naomi then became God's vessel for what He had intended to happen.

So, for a little while longer they had to wait upon the Lord, but their multiple blessings did come. Ruth was blessed with a newfound husband, child, and prosperity and Naomi with a new grandson as their lineage extended itself and life went on. Ruth had shown obedience not only to her mother-in-law but most importantly, to God Himself. Without listening to Naomi, there's no telling where she may have wound up.

Such a decision should be the same for which we as His children should do. Be obedient and listen to God's instruction and teaching us about how we should proceed in our day to day lives according to the Lord. We should also be aware of the fact that sometimes, God uses others to convey His words and produce His outcomes. Therefore, we should make ourselves more open to others close to us and listen.

God had His eyes on the prizes for both women as well as Boaz. Had any of these characters differed in her or his approach to God's calling and discernment of spirit in wisdom and opportunities availing themselves, then all might have had misgivings and missed the mark to their own individual blessings as guided by the Lord. This is something that we all need to think about and reflect upon in our own lives.

Sometimes, our patience grows thin in the challenges which are set before us and we proceed unshielded from prosperity and danger simply because we think we can; therefore, we do it our way without any thought about, "What would God have directed us to do had we relied upon His word?" Do we alone set most of our own obstacles right before our very eyes because we refuse to submit to the will of God? God most certainly instructed Ruth as to what was the way to go while guiding her with His eye.

Are we willing to wait for the prize according to our Savior like Ruth and Naomi? Or will we continue walking blindly forth alone? Can we even fathom what the Lord will reveal unto us in our walk with Him? Also, can we thank Him for His grace and mercy and patience in our matters?

Revelation: God awaits a prize for certain for all of us who are faithful to Him.

Endeavor: Thank you for helping us learn to wait a little while longer in wisdom for our blessings.

Prayer: Help us to wisely follow Your prescribed protocol, Lord, as did your daughter Ruth in the instructing, hearing, and listening of Your words as You then guided her with Your eyes. Certainly, several truths regarding the wisdom and character of Ruth must have been witnessed and revealed to Naomi from Ruth which she followed and obeyed accordingly. Amen.

A MATTER OF TIME

*Finally, brethren, whatsoever things are true, whatsoever
things are honest, whatsoever things are just, whatsoever
things are pure, whatsoever things are lovely, whatsoever
things are of good report; if there be any virtue, and
if there be any praise, think on these things.*

| PHILIPPIANS 4:8

Regarding the current imprisonment of Paul which followed after his
shipwreck because prior to that time when he was speaking to the
people with his apostles, Caesar ruled across his lands and he thought
that Paul was trying to overtake him and start an insurrection against
his rule. One must remember that prior to Paul's exaltation to apostle
himself as a follower of Christ, he had done some pretty ugly things in
persecuting Christians. Possibly, too wicked to imagine.

Paul leaped out on faith and began preaching and teaching according
to how God had instructed him to minister. It is amazing the beauty
for which he still experienced in humanity and nature over a matter of
time as it formed, grew, and developed into his letter to the brethren
at Philippi. I often wonder what and how the brethren reacted to the
words of this man of God. Had they wondered if his words were in a
message from God Himself, or if some kind of spiritual awakening had
overcome him?

Therefore, Paul believed that his brethren should think, reflect,
and act accordingly from his letter when it came to virtue; exhibiting
good moral character and praise; attesting admiration or adoration to be

presented to God, and justice in following his teaching to his apostles. Truly, Paul was a man of his words and most especially, God's words. He makes us look into our own hearts to discern the simplicities of life and to tell of a simpler life. One of time, leisure, beauty, wisdom, miracles, and humility to ourselves and one another in admiration.

When I think of the words in the above verse, I see them just as clearly being associated with the following things in today's world as well as was existent during Paul's time period. Whatsoever things are true, a good friend. Honest, a young child. Just, a fair attorney. Pure, a newborn baby. Lovely, a beautiful flower. Being of good report, a faithful student. And he closes with if there be any virtue or praise, to think on them. Such innocence in the midst and essence of each thing which he poses for not only the people of his time but for our time as well.

How often in our daily walk with God have we failed to be a disciple of His spreading the sanctified goodness, greatness, and glory which lay in in the simplest of words and things here on earth? If we individually would think upon Paul's words, what could we envision for God's people? Do his words seem somehow differently flavored as he writes from his prison cell or should we possibly, not expect such purity, serenity, humbleness, and gentility for such a man as he based on his past? A past which was not sought by love of God or country necessarily, but by his own wants and means.

Revelation: May we seek to know through wisdom and enjoy the simplest pleasures in life.

Endeavor: Willingness to learn God's plan for our lives in a matter of time.

Prayer: Enable Your people to favorably act on behalf of others in God's time. May we remember simple times in our lives such as a picnic basket, barbecues, hiking trails, riding bikes, reading poetry, playing in the creek and pitching horseshoes. Thus, infusing the words, thoughts, and visions of Paul today and forever more in our hearts. Amen.

WISDOM BROTHER

Deliver me in thy righteousness, and cause me to escape: incline thine ear unto me, and save me.

PSALM 71:2

There are many times in our lives, even while governed by God and the courts that man has made mistakes, taken missteps, and/or fallen short of the glory of God. Certainly, many of whom have fallen down and prostrated their souls while at the cross of mercy for our Lord. Some in the Bible were named accordingly as Adam, Cain, Abraham, Saul, Moses, Hezekiah, Noah, Jonah, Matthew, and Peter.

But there have been times and situations too numerous to fully recite and dwell upon in the Bible which leave us almost breathless in speech and function when it comes to the wisdom of our brother Job, in Christ. He was at times, seen as profound and renowned in scope and size better known as big in today's times.

It seems that Job was one of the most fortunate servants of God who was amazingly amassed with an overabundance in wealth, fame, and fortune. Why one could say that he was blessed beyond measure and highly favored among men in the Bible by the Lord, our God as he was seen as one who walked perfectly and upright, fearing the Lord and resisting evil.

Talking about favor. Why he and his wife had multiple children and lineage, servants, multitudes of cattle, camels, barns, mansions as homesteads, and his children had their own homes and lived like royalty upon the earth. That was how favored he was by the Lord.

One day as Satan came along with the sons of God to dwell before the Lord, he was given the proposition by God to challenge the faith, obedience, and wisdom of Job. Satan had felt that God had sheltered Job and his family to the point that no harm would ever befall them in their lives.

But God allowed the hedge of protection to be taken away from Job and in that he began having losses. Losses of family, sheep, oxen, and asses as cattle, houses and so forth. It was to the point that Job had sores upon his body which he tried to scrape as they ravished his soul and his wife told him to curse the Lord for all of His misfortunes to their family. Satan of course remained an instigator in the mess for months.

Job of course refused, however made it plain to the Lord, that he did not understand all of what was happening to him as he had been a faithful servant unto the Lord and would continuously bless His name. He did become so humiliated and shamed that he cursed the day in which he was born. Luckily, his three friends came from afar to mourn, comfort, and pray with him in his travails. All cried out in not recognizing this great man of God who was so grieved and afflicted physically, mentally, and spiritually. He was to the point where he had almost forgotten about the hedge of protection which God had given him and all that he stood for.

Certainly, all of this time in which Job was being tried was long and drawn out. It must have been a time of pure hell and nightmares during both the day and night for Job, wondering when and if everything that had befallen him would come to a desired end in his life and his wife's. Days and nights seemed long and arduous for him and remembering the omnipotence of God.

He probably slept praying for divine intervention in listening for God's voice and deliverance from his trespasses and transgressions upon his life; somehow finding a way to escape, and save himself. Still, he acted faithfully and grew in wisdom with the Lord as he came to realize not to take anything for granted. Gifts and favor that had been previously granted, did not mean they were meant for lifelong happiness as he too soon discovered.

There were so many unanswered questions and concerns which Job accumulated over months of time wondering just when everything would end, and if he'd ever resume normally in his life again. Such heartache and pain and derision which he bore, but not without Satan on his trail which Job was not oblivious to as each breath he counted and thanked the Lord.

In the end, for Job's stalwart faithfulness, graven wisdom, and bolden favor with God… he was rewarded two times over for what he had lost and lived to see four generations of his lineage living a hundred and forty years. Quite amazing for one man to experience and others to witness!

How many of us can say that we would be willing to walk the walk and talk the talk as Job had to his distracters who were many against the promises of God? Also, how many of us would be willing to make such sacrifices and then be open to the wisdom which we accumulated to try to understand the tribulations we had gone through or were currently still in?

Revelation: Understand and know that we can be faithful servants of God even today.

Endeavor: Through all of our life's circumstances, may we grow in wisdom as our brother Job to know the grandeur of the Lord.

Prayer: During all of the temptations of Satan against us, may we remember You, Lord. Also, may God deliver us from any unrighteousness, protect and save us as He did Job. For surely there shall be the naysayers and haters who swarm around us and only want our failures, losses, and misbelief unveiled amongst the masses to then proclaim us as heathens and evil-doers of our God. Amen.

REFLECTIONS FROM YESTERDAY

My son, if thou wilt receive my words, and hide my commandments
with thee; So that thou incline thine ear unto wisdom, and
apply thine heart to understanding; Yea, if thou criest after
knowledge, and liftest up thy voice for understanding; If
thou seekest her as silver, and searchest for her as for hid
treasures; Then shalt thou understand the fear of the Lord,
and find the knowledge of God. For the Lord giveth wisdom: out
of His mouth cometh knowledge and understanding.

PROVERBS 2:1-6

Each new day of living offers us reflections from yesterday. Reflections based on our morals, beliefs, education or lack thereof, monetary resources or lack thereof, health status, and varied negotiations found in all facets of our living and learning experiences. We have the God-given ability to assess each of the above criteria with our own set of standards and values to either ignore and/or improve our individual human conditions for tomorrow.

Likewise, we can choose to get professional medical services and mental health assistance to be in concert with helping us to discern our Christian values. Following, we can proceed to use the knowledge, understanding, and wisdom which we have accrued from God in making critical decisions in our reflections from yesterday. Reflections for whom instant moments allow us to remember for a lifetime but can come and go in a glance as simple as that.

As summarized from the above scriptures, listening to the Lord and following His commandments will incline one to grow and find wisdom and apply understanding to the knowledge which one seeks as it comes from out of God's mouth likened to silver and hidden treasures. Of course, what does one do but polish the silver and hearken the treasures in one's heart literally if they are obedient to God's will.

Sometimes, we don't want to look at our yesterdays as they may show or exhibit our many weaknesses versus strengths. But in order to grow stronger in our daily lives, we must assess where we currently stand overall in all things today to be better for our tomorrows. May the Lord help us to determine our goals from this day forward as we lean into Him for applicable wisdom. Wisdom which defined means adding insight by discernment into one's inner qualities and relationships.

Just like in the Bible where Jesus talks to His disciples and gives them information to use in obtaining knowledge, understanding and wisdom in their sojourns across the lands aiding and healing the masses of people to the glory of God. They understood the fear and reverence for the Lord. Such reflections added to their mission of restoring sight to the blind, allowing the lame to walk, and the dead to live again amongst other gifts.

Exactly, what might we glean from yesterday and bygone years in our meaning of today in our lives? Can we honestly attest to the glory and wisdom of the Lord being allowed by us to guide us in our understanding of today and tomorrow? Or do we just sit idly by and let things be as they are with no connection to how our futures will be tomorrow? How will we know that we have acquired wisdom as given by God? What would we look for to guide us?

Revelation: We have learned that through acquiring knowledge and getting a good understanding of something, that we have gained wisdom in that area.

Endeavor: We need to assess our lives to make changes today for a better day tomorrow.

Prayer: As written above, the Lord gives wisdom and out of His mouth comes knowledge and understanding. We must know then that such wisdom, knowledge, and understanding does not just present themselves to us but grows in time…possibly over the course of a long life in fact. Help us to come face to face with ourselves and look at our reflections from yesterday. If we need to make changes, do it Amen.

POETRY

GRAY HATRED

Hatred... stared me in the eyes a year ago today
on my Amtrak journey from Chicago to Battle Creek.
Quickly, I turned my back away from its rude ugliness
not allowing such another glance to take from my essence.

It... wasn't easy as it proceeded; forcefully ricocheting itself
towards my face in a semi-quasi, militant front.
Bewildered, I was aghast at the level of gray hatred
literally searing in such instantaneous moments at me.

Volleying... back and forth continuously into its main court,
the hatred remained non-conciliatory and confrontational.
Anxiously, I felt its sting as if I were a player in a game
on a worn-out court; losing significantly to the challenger.

Smiling... I tried to retreat and greet hatred; sending it back to
its home court as it unwittingly persevered in playing
hardball again and again across the net and way beyond my reach
as I began trembling profusely from all of the drama at hand.

Determined... that hatred hadn't won, I turned around and picked up my
briefcase from the floor; taking the laptop out from its case and gently
laying it across the small table before me I began simply writing
about its unknown origin of rage and ignorance on this most beautiful day.

Written by Donna Collier Rickman

MASKED STORIES

Wooden-carved masks... many, sculpted from

mahogany,

walnut,

oak,

ebony,

cedar,

and white pine Tree Barks.

Elegantly-adorned... simply-set in

jewels,

beads,

metals,

wires,

paints.

and cloths Beautifully-Colored.

Symbolically-constructed... telling stories of

marriages,

fertilities,

deaths,

wars,

celebrations,

and rites of passages Within Cultures.

Because it had been stated long ago...

each mask...once passed

from the hands of its original maker

reveals its own face,

finds its own place,

and creates its own story to be told...

each time it's passed onto a new owner.

Whether from shaman to medicine man...

from grandparent to parent...

from parent to child,

from villager to villager,

traveler to traveler,

from sales shop owner to garage sale owner...

until landing into its newest hands.

For what one sees, imagines, and hears from the mask...

may be quite different to another handling the very same

mask therefore, be ready to watch and listen.

Let the spirit of the masks share their own stories...

revealing their own truths to you as you handle

their inherent uniqueness and

respect their ultimate wisdom.

Written by Donna Collier Rickman

SITTING AMONGST MY SISTERS

Sitting amongst my sisters, I am truly honored, delighted, humbled, and proud feeling encircled by their love, protection, works, and strength throughout the years as I have situated... a plethora of their writings bound in books of poetry, narratives, anthologies and magazines throughout my 1894 Victorian home.

Maya Angelo, Niki Giovanni, and Gwendolyn Brooks sit on the fireplace mantle as Oprah Winfrey, Alice Walker, and Toni Morrison lie on my living room table... while Sojourner Truth, Frances Ellen Watkins Harper, Harriet Tubman, Ida B. Wells, and Lucy Terry Prince stand on the organ shelves in my parlor.

To name just a few of the giants whom I admire in both prose and poetry's history, I am taken back to a time when African-American women weren't legitimately recognized as phenomenal writers... not able to praise or speak and write onto paper the truth of their words sewn deep into the flesh of their hearts and etched into the pictures of their minds.

Such women were not allowed by society to be all that God had called them to become, or that they ever wanted to be, yearning to rise up to such standards birthed within them... even though they knew in their souls that their words were predestined for greatness given by God as His vessels, tools, and instruments of truth to all who would read and listen.

But let the status quo assume its role in trying to erase their voices as set forth in societal, and political circles during unpreceded events in history and the above such will never happen because their essences and influences are all too powerfully encapsulating.... within the African-American pulse of our culture and customs honoring their contributions.

May we all as Americans...mostly immigrants to this country, learn to seek those diverse voices which speak out in pen and verse to the truths which they see and envision happening within the core of our roots, family values, and cultures that embodies them and their gifts, talents, and sacrifices for which this nation has rested its laurels on, prayed for, and offered up to others.

Written by Donna Collier Rickman

SEASONAL MOON TIDES

MOON of THREE Fates (Moirai)...
"My tether lines have been
divinely spun and apportioned;
unsnapped by my creator, God.

MOON of multiple births...
winked its watchful, large eyes;
smiling upon my twin brother and our deliveries
under the Ram's thirtieth moonlight.

MOON of AFFECTIVE SEASONAL DISORDER...
saturates post-menopausal hormones;
riding the high and low icy-white,
tides fluctuating within my soul.

MOON of the Hazelnut...
about the size of a squirrel's ear;
blanketing my fertile garden's flower beds
filled with hybrid seeds and heirloom bulbs.

MOON of the RISING WATER'S Run-offs...
quenching my budding plants' thirsts;
bursting forth their many heads of hair in opulent,
multi-colored lengths, textures and designs.

MOON of my Mother's Tether Line...
was finally snipped to freedom by our God;

DONNA COLLIER RICKMAN

battling the life-long effects of an inherited disease,
her spirit flies freely amongst my colorful, decoupage.

MOON of FAMILY REUNIONS...
preparing barbecued meats, salads, baked beans, and greens;
playing card games, checkers, horseshoes, and badminton
continues our family's tradition while drinking cool lemonade.

MOON of Children's Innocence...
Seasoned by children's excitement and laughter;
born using pencils, crayons, markers, and journals,
they are prompted as Jr. authors to creatively write.

MOON of TEACHER's REFLECTIONS...
filled with sleepless nights, organization, lesson planning,
grading papers, and tests in anticipation for
preparation into the new school year.

MOON of the Full Twilight...
as it lights up the night and roars in laughter;
glaring its fiery eyes and meeting the many costumed
trick or treaters at my haunted-house doorsteps.

MOON of THANKFULNESS...
bringing family and friends sitting closely together;
eating plenty of home-cooked foods and comforting,
baked pies and cakes, blessed with much prayer.

MOON of Jesus' birth...
our saving grace and salvation, Christmas carols inter-mixed
with candy canes, cookies, gingerbread houses, presents,
and dear ole' Saint Nick's promises for peace and happiness.

Written by Donna Collier Rickman

EPILOGUE

Upfront and initially, I want to say that God, my Heavenly Father was forever present in my thoughts guiding my writings (in all genres) as inspirational works from Him from the very beginnings to the end. Literally, He took my fingers and ran with them playing gospel, classical, jazz, R&B, and country music on the computer keys. Truly, there were ups and downs, jolts and thrusts, pins and pricks, and otherwise some unusually smooth rides into my soul of righteousness.

Next, I want to thank four authors: T. D. Jakes, Women Thou Art Loosed, Parker J. Palmer, Let Your life Speak. Iyanla Vanzant, Faith In the Valley and the late Dorothy A. Kemp, Lingering Impressions for their most valuable writing forms and impressions upon me. All played substantially into the writing of this book from their personal essays, memoirs, and meditations. Equally, each spoke of changes and challenges for what they felt their reading audience as well themselves endured and what seemed for why the world needed to read their works. I cannot thank them enough believing that they were my mentors in this endeavor.

When I first began writing this book, I was consumed with issues that had only been affecting my life. I felt like God had blessed me to endure and overcome the pain and uncertainties... thus share such victories with the world. And so, what I did was basically take a telescopic look at those issues and or people who had played significant roles making a difference in my life to then write about us in memoirs or personal essays.

From broadening outward from just my own perspective, I began to look at how the world issues in particular had contributed equally as well, if not more and wondered also, how had various characters from the Bible dealt with their particular challenges and overcome. So, I then challenged myself into that quest of writing meditations based on the scriptures.

I had been privy to write poetry during various times of my life and decided that choosing some of them which happened during some unusually, crucial times in my life as well as family and or friend's lives could thus become beneficial to the readers especially while in discussions having read them between the entries or at the end of the book readings.

I admit that my writings many times became utterances which reverberated into my heart and soul. It is like I can feel, see, and hear what others are thinking and feeling inside to understand their reasonings for what they thought were justifications for their actions. However, in the end of the story God had the final say for what did actually occur or go down in their lives.

And finally, with each entry lie the talking points of discussions through the commentary, revelations, prayers, and endeavors to allow readers their opportunities to reach out to Christ and grow in spirituality with one's Maker and others possibly through a reader's group at home, church, or within one's community. To God be the glory! It can't be stated enough.

Donna Collier Rickman

INDEX

277, 286, 309, 313, 314, 327, 332, 333, 341

F

falling down 62, 168
false idols 278
family ix, 11, 21, 34, 39, 41, 42, 43, 47, 51, 64, 65, 66, 67, 72, 79, 80, 87, 89, 94, 104, 117, 122, 133, 136, 138, 141, 145, 146, 152, 153, 154, 163, 168, 173, 174, 181, 184, 186, 198, 204, 205, 212, 224, 225, 226, 227, 261, 265, 269, 270, 273, 292, 297, 302, 309, 311, 318, 331, 333, 336
Fibromyalgia 56, 57
foundations 1, 51, 216, 217
freedom 1, 81, 83, 84, 87, 89, 90, 94, 95, 138, 145, 219, 280, 281, 290, 332, 342
friendship 147, 148, 215

G

George Floyd 74, 75

H

Harriet Tubman 115, 330
holidays 269, 270, 344
homelessness 1, 254

I

imprisonment 88, 89, 90, 315

J

Job 1, 17, 19, 42, 44, 45, 51, 54, 56, 57, 58, 65, 79, 80, 115, 120, 136, 195, 212, 214, 229, 261, 268, 289, 317, 318, 319, 342

L

leaves 2, 7, 17, 22, 39, 45, 50, 63, 103, 104, 184, 205, 221, 222, 244, 262, 297, 300, 309, 317, 342

M

Mandela 88, 89, 90, 280, 281
marital union 173, 177, 313
mental health 7, 57, 209, 229, 262, 266, 321
Moses 115, 161, 162, 163, 271, 272, 277, 278, 317
Mother Teresa 266

N

Noah 301, 302, 303, 317

O

old souls 311, 312, 345

P

patience 88, 93, 94, 95, 133, 134, 138, 207, 209, 210, 211, 212, 213, 310, 314, 343
people ii, iii, 23, 26, 33, 34, 41, 50, 51, 53, 60, 65, 66, 74, 75, 80, 84, 86, 88, 89, 103, 105, 115, 119, 122, 123, 127, 137, 138, 145, 146, 149, 150, 159, 161, 162, 164, 165, 166, 178, 179, 180, 182, 194, 198, 199, 200, 205, 223, 224, 229, 246, 247, 260, 261, 262, 265, 266, 269, 271, 272, 274, 277, 278, 279, 281, 291, 297, 298, 304, 305, 313, 315, 316, 322, 335, 343
physical health 7
pregnancy 26, 179, 184, 198, 258
prosperity 75, 86, 87, 313, 314, 342

FUTHER READINGS AND GUIDED DISCUSSIONS

ANXIOUSNESS:
Listless Moods --- Psalm 119:26-30
Wandering Spirit --- Philippians 4:4-7
Sojourning Another Day --- I Peter 4:12-19
Delicate Eyes --- Isaiah 41:8-13

DISOBEDIENCE:
Ignorant Decisions --- Isaiah 30:20-22
Not My Brother's Keeper --- Genesis 4:1-15
Lost At Sea --- Jonah 1:17, 2:1, 10
Redemption Through Jesus Christ --- Ezekiel 18:20-28

EXALTATION:
Beautifully Made --- Psalm 139:13-17
Mixed Betrayal --- Matthew 27:1-18
Knight In Shining Armor --- II Samuel 17:1-58
Surely Ready --- Philippians 2:1-11
Not My Will Lord --- James 1:1-10
Forget Me Not --- I Peter 5:1-10

FAITH:
Wake Us Everyone --- Acts 16:9-31
How Great Thou Art --- St. Matthew 9:20-22
Be Done With It --- St. James 4:6-10
I'm On My Way --- Proverbs 18:1-10

Charting Waters --- St. Mark 4:35-41
Abiding Faith --- II Corinthians 4:7-11
Our Douglasville Community --- II Timothy 3:10-17

FORGIVENESS
Tender Care Always --- Ephesians 4:29-32
Blistering Frills --- Ephesians 4:1-6
Save It For Another Day --- I Peter 5:1-8
Simply Speaking --- St. Luke 17:1-6

FREEDOM
Feathers Of A Bird --- Galatians 5:1-6
Prosperity Not Shame In The Lord --- Jeremiah 29:1-13
Run The Race --- II Corinthians 6:1-10
Walking The Lighthouse Stairs --- St. James --- 1:1-18

GRACE
Rustling Leaves --- St. John 15:1-9
Sit Still And Listen --- II Corinthians 12:1-10
Two cups Of Coffee --- St. John 14:23-28
Amazing Grace --- Provers 3:1-8

HOPE
Stalwart Confidence --- Job 11:13-20
Until We Meet Again --- St. John 11:21-46
Beating Down Sun --- II Corinthians 5:10-21
Quite Frankly --- II Timothy 1:1-12
Finding My Pen --- I Peter 4:11-14, 19
Turning Point ---Jeremiah 29:11-13

JOY
Resounding Joy --- St. James 1:2-8
Rising Sun --- Psalm 113:3-9
Laughing Again --- Psalm 126: 1-6
Roll Them Up --- Psalm 106:1-5

LOVE
Love Heals All --- I Corinthians 13: 1-8
Between Friends --- St. John 14: 13-18
Loving You Is Beautiful --- St. John 14:15
Eating Together --- Deuteronomy 11: 8-22

LOYALTY
Withering Heights --- St. John 3:13-18
Just A Closer Walk ---Exodus 33:13-23
Some People ---Titus 3:1-11
Fear Thou Not --- Isaiah 41:1-10

MARRIAGE
Covenant Kiss --- Ephesians 5:20-31
Small Sips of Tea --- Esther 2:16-21
The Odd Couple --- Genesis 17:15-19
Righteous Living ---St. Luke 1:5-26
One Name Only ---St. Luke 1:26-38
Unearned Favor --- Genesis 2:18-25

OBEDIENCE:
Listening Intently --- James 1:19-26
Whispering Raindrops --- Leviticus 26: 3-9
Blessed Servant Of God ---Judges 4:4-24
Blessings Forevermore --- Philippians 2:13-16
Be At Attention --- Romans 8:24-39
Smile when You're Happy Psalm 106:1-6

PATIENCE:
Patient Favor --- St. James 1:1-6
Patience My Child --- Galatians 6:6-10
Slowly Brewing --- Jeremiah 29:8-14
Standing On Shaky Ground --- St. Luke 6:41-49

Short-Tailed Feathers --- Genesis 8:1-12
Casting One's Cares --- Psalm 37:1-11

<u>WISDOM</u>
Glorious Principles --- Proverbs 19: 5-11
An Old Soul --- Proverbs 2: 1-6
A Little While Longer --- Psalm 32:4-8
A Matter of Time --- I Philippians 4:6-8
Wisdom Brother --- Psalm 71:1-6
Reflections From Yesterday ---Proverbs 2:1-11

BIBLIOGRAPHY

Vanzant, Iyanla. *Faith In The Valley*. Fireside Rockefeller Center, Simon & Schuster, New York, New York, 1996.

Countryman, J. *God's Promises & Answers For Your Life*. A division of Thomas Nelson, Inc., Nashville, Tennessee, 1999.

Palmer, Parker J. *Let Your Life Speak (Listening for the Voice of Vocation)*. Jossey-Bass Inc., San Francisco, California, 2000.

Hahn, Jennifer. *Light For My Path*. Humble Creek, Barbour Publishing, Inc., Uhrichsville, Ohio, 2002.

Kemp, Dorothy A. *Lingering Impressions*. Moose Enterprise Book and Theatre Play Publishing Moose Hide Books, Sault Ste. Marie, Ontario, Canada, 2005.

The Holy Bible (King James Version). Elm Hill Press, 1977.

Jakes, T.D. *The Holy Bible, Woman Thou Art Loosed! Edition*. Thomas Nelson, Inc., Nashville, Tennessee, 1998.

The Living Bible Promise Book. Barbour and Company Inc., 1971.

Merriam-Webster.com. Merriam Webster, 2022.

Wikipedia.org. Wikipedia, 2022.

NOTECARDS